The Ultimate Pie Cookbook

Dishes, Volume 6

Olivia Bennett

Published by B&H Publishing Group, 2025.

THE ULTIMATE PIE COOKBOOK

First edition. February 22, 2025.

Copyright © 2025 Olivia Bennett.

ISBN: 979-8230959069

Written by Olivia Bennett.

Table of Contents

To all the home bakers, pie lovers, and kitchen adventurers—this book
is for you.

To my family and friends, whose laughter and love have filled my
kitchen as much as the scent of freshly baked pies.

And to everyone who believes that a warm slice of pie has the power to
bring people together—may your crusts be flaky, your fillings rich, and
your memories sweet.

Introduction: The Timeless Appeal of Pies

Pies hold a special place in the culinary world, transcending cultures, cuisines, and generations. From flaky crusts encasing warm, spiced apples to golden pastry pockets filled with savory meats, pies offer something for every palate and occasion. They are symbols of home, comfort, and celebration, evoking memories of family gatherings, holidays, and cherished traditions. This chapter delves into the rich history and cultural significance of pies, explores why they continue to captivate our hearts and taste buds, and provides an overview of the diverse recipes and techniques included in this book.

The History of Pies: A Journey Through Time

Ancient Origins

Pies have been enjoyed for millennia, with their origins tracing back to ancient civilizations.

1. The Egyptians:
   - The earliest known pies date to ancient Egypt around 9500 BC.
   - These pies featured simple crusts made from oat, wheat, or barley and were filled with honey or nuts.
2. The Greeks:
   - Ancient Greeks developed pastry shells to encase meat and seafood.
   - They referred to these creations as "artocreas," marking the beginning of savory pies.
3. The Romans:
   - Romans refined pie-making by using a pastry shell called "pasta" to preserve and transport fillings.
   - Their recipes included meats, fruits, and spices, showcasing the versatility of pies.

Medieval Evolution

During the Middle Ages, pies gained popularity across Europe, becoming both a practical and celebratory dish.

1. Practicality:

- Pies were used to preserve food, as the thick crust acted as a container to seal in ingredients.

- They were often filled with meats and spices to mask spoilage.

2. Festive Feasts:

- Pies became a centerpiece for feasts and banquets, with elaborate designs and decorative crusts.

- Sweet pies, such as fruit tarts and custard pies, emerged during this period.

The Renaissance and Beyond

The Renaissance brought refinement to pie-making, with more sophisticated ingredients and techniques.

1. Influence of Trade:

- Spices like cinnamon, nutmeg, and cloves, introduced through trade routes, enhanced pie fillings.

- Sugar became more accessible, leading to the rise of sweet dessert pies.

2. Colonial America:

- European settlers brought pie traditions to America, adapting recipes to include indigenous ingredients like pumpkins, pecans, and cranberries.

- Pies became a symbol of American ingenuity and resourcefulness.

Modern-Day Pies

Today, pies are celebrated globally, with each culture contributing its unique twist.

1. British Pies: Steak and kidney pie, Cornish pasties.

2. French Pies: Quiches, tarte Tatin.

3. American Pies: Apple pie, key lime pie, pecan pie.

4. Global Variations: Empanadas in Latin America, samosas in India, and b'stilla in Morocco.

Why Pies Are the Ultimate Comfort Food

1. Nostalgia and Tradition

Pies are deeply tied to memories of home, family, and special occasions. A warm apple pie cooling on the windowsill or a pumpkin pie gracing the Thanksgiving table evokes feelings of warmth and togetherness.

2. Versatility

Pies can be sweet or savory, simple or elaborate, and suitable for any occasion. From a hearty chicken pot pie on a cold winter night to a refreshing fruit tart on a summer afternoon, pies adapt to every need.

3. Sensory Delight

Pies engage all the senses:

- The flaky, buttery crust provides a satisfying crunch.

- The aroma of baked fruit or spiced fillings creates anticipation.

- The vibrant colors and decorative designs add visual appeal.

4. Universal Appeal

Pies transcend cultural and dietary boundaries. Whether filled with meats, vegetables, fruits, or creams, there's a pie for everyone.

Overview of the Book

This book is your comprehensive guide to mastering the art of pie-making. From traditional favorites to innovative twists, you'll find recipes and techniques to suit every occasion. Here's what you can expect:

Part 1: Mastering the Basics

We begin with the fundamentals:

- Chapter 1: The secrets to a perfect pie crust, from flaky all-butter recipes to gluten-free alternatives.

- Chapter 2: How to tailor crusts for sweet or savory fillings.

- Chapter 3: Essential tools and techniques, from latticework to decorative edges.

Part 2: Classic Sweet Pies

This section celebrates timeless sweet pies:

- Chapter 4: Seasonal fruit pies, like apple and cherry, to highlight nature's bounty.

- Chapter 5: Creamy and custard pies, offering silky textures and indulgent flavors.

- Chapter 6: Decadent chocolate pies for rich, satisfying desserts.

- Chapter 7: Holiday classics, like pumpkin and pecan pie, that bring families together.

Part 3: Savory Pies

Explore hearty, meal-worthy pies:

- Chapter 8: Classic pot pies filled with meats and vegetables.
- Chapter 9: Quiches and tarts, perfect for brunch or light dinners.
- Chapter 10: Regional meat pies from around the world.

Part 4: Modern and Creative Pies

For those looking to push boundaries:

- Chapter 11: No-bake pies that are quick, easy, and delicious.
- Chapter 12: Hand pies and mini pies for on-the-go snacking.
- Chapter 13: Vegan and gluten-free options for modern dietary needs.

Part 5: Pies for Special Occasions

End with show-stopping creations:

- Chapter 14: Decorative party pies that impress guests.
- Chapter 15: Frozen and ice cream pies for refreshing desserts.

Celebrating the Joy of Pie-Making

Pie-making is an act of love and creativity. It's about taking simple ingredients and transforming them into something extraordinary. Whether you're rolling dough for the first time or crafting intricate latticework, every pie tells a story.

It's a way to express care, celebrate milestones, and share a piece of yourself with those you love.

This book invites you to embark on a journey through the world of pies. With its rich history, comforting flavors, and endless possibilities, pie-making is more than a skill—it's a lifelong passion. So roll up your sleeves, dust your counter with flour, and get ready to create something truly special. The world of pies awaits!

Chapter 1: The Art of the Perfect Pie Crust

A great pie crust is the foundation of any exceptional pie. It's the crisp, flaky exterior that cradles your filling, adding texture and flavor while holding everything together. Achieving the perfect pie crust is a skill every baker should master, and with the right tools, techniques, and recipes, it's easier than you might think.

In this chapter, we'll explore the essential ingredients and tools for creating flaky, tender crusts, dive into techniques like rolling, chilling, and blind baking, and provide step-by-step recipes for classic all-butter crusts, shortening crusts, and gluten-free alternatives. By the end, you'll have everything you need to confidently craft the perfect crust for any pie.

The Essentials of a Perfect Pie Crust

Key Ingredients

The simplicity of pie crusts is part of their beauty. With just a few ingredients, you can create a masterpiece—but each component must be handled with care.

1. Flour

Flour is the backbone of any pie crust, providing structure and stability.

- All-Purpose Flour: The most versatile option for pie crusts, balancing protein content for structure and tenderness.

- Pastry Flour: Lower in protein, resulting in a softer, more delicate crust. Ideal for dessert pies.

- Gluten-Free Flour Blends: For those avoiding gluten, these blends mimic the properties of traditional flours.

2. Fat

Fat is the key to creating a flaky, tender crust. It coats the flour, preventing gluten development, and melts during baking to create air pockets.

- Butter: Adds flavor and creates flaky layers. Use unsalted butter for better control of seasoning.

- Shortening: Produces exceptionally tender crusts and is easy to work with due to its higher melting point.

- Lard: Offers a rich flavor and unbeatable flakiness, often used in savory pies.

- Coconut Oil: A plant-based option that works well in vegan or dairy-free crusts.

3. Liquid

Liquid brings the dough together. The key is to use just enough to bind the ingredients without making the dough too wet.

- Ice Water: Keeps the dough cold, preventing the fat from melting prematurely.

- Vinegar or Lemon Juice: A small splash can help inhibit gluten formation, resulting in a tender crust.

- Milk or Cream: Adds richness and a golden hue to the baked crust.

4. Salt and Sugar

- Salt: Enhances flavor and balances sweetness.

- Sugar: Optional, but adds a touch of sweetness and helps with browning in dessert crusts.

Essential Tools

Investing in the right tools can make pie crust preparation smoother and more enjoyable.

1. Pastry Cutter or Food Processor: For cutting fat into flour quickly and evenly.

2. Rolling Pin: A classic wooden rolling pin is ideal for rolling out dough.

3. Pastry Mat or Parchment Paper: Helps prevent sticking and makes cleanup easier.

4. Pie Weights: Keeps the crust flat during blind baking.

5. Bench Scraper: Useful for gathering and handling dough.

6. Pie Dish: Metal, glass, or ceramic options each provide different baking results.

Techniques for a Perfect Pie Crust

1. Cutting the Fat

The process of cutting fat into flour is crucial for achieving a flaky crust. The goal is to create pea-sized pieces of fat that will melt during baking, creating pockets of air.

- By Hand: Use a pastry cutter or your fingers to work the fat into the flour.
- Food Processor: Pulse the fat and flour briefly to achieve an even consistency.

2. Mixing and Hydrating

Once the fat is incorporated, gradually add cold liquid. Use a fork or your hands to gently mix the dough until it just comes together. Avoid overmixing, as this can lead to a tough crust.

3. Chilling the Dough

Chilling is non-negotiable. It allows the gluten to relax and the fat to firm up, making the dough easier to handle and preventing shrinkage during baking.

- Wrap the dough in plastic wrap and chill for at least 30 minutes, or up to 24 hours.

4. Rolling Out the Dough

When rolling, aim for a uniform thickness of about 1/8 inch. Keep these tips in mind:

- Flour your surface and rolling pin lightly to prevent sticking.
- Roll from the center outward, rotating the dough frequently to maintain a circular shape.

5. Transferring the Dough

Gently roll the dough onto your rolling pin or fold it into quarters to transfer it to the pie dish. Press it lightly into the corners and trim any excess.

6. Blind Baking

Blind baking is essential for pies with fillings that don't require baking (e.g., cream pies) or those that need a partially baked crust (e.g., quiches).

Steps:

1. Line the crust with parchment paper or foil.

2. Fill with pie weights or dried beans.

3. Bake at 375°F for 15-20 minutes, then remove weights and bake for an additional 5-10 minutes until golden.

Pie Crust Recipes

1. Classic All-Butter Pie Crust

This recipe produces a flavorful, flaky crust perfect for both sweet and savory pies.

Ingredients:

- 2 1/2 cups all-purpose flour
- 1 teaspoon salt
- 1 teaspoon sugar (optional)
- 1 cup (2 sticks) unsalted butter, cold and cubed
- 6-8 tablespoons ice water

Instructions:

1. In a large bowl, whisk together flour, salt, and sugar.

2. Add butter and cut into the flour until the mixture resembles coarse crumbs.

3. Gradually add ice water, one tablespoon at a time, mixing until the dough just comes together.

4. Divide the dough in half, shape into discs, and wrap in plastic wrap. Chill for at least 30 minutes.

2. Shortening Pie Crust

A go-to for tender, easy-to-handle crusts.

Ingredients:

- 2 1/2 cups all-purpose flour

- 1 teaspoon salt
- 1 cup vegetable shortening
- 6-8 tablespoons ice water

Instructions:

1. Combine flour and salt in a bowl.
2. Cut in shortening until the mixture resembles small peas.
3. Add ice water gradually, mixing until the dough comes together.
4. Form into discs, wrap, and chill as directed.

3. Gluten-Free Pie Crust

This crust is tender and flaky, suitable for those avoiding gluten.

Ingredients:

- 2 cups gluten-free flour blend
- 1 teaspoon xanthan gum (if not included in the blend)
- 1 teaspoon sugar
- 1/2 teaspoon salt
- 1/2 cup unsalted butter or shortening, cold and cubed
- 1 egg
- 2-4 tablespoons ice water

Instructions:

1. Mix flour, xanthan gum, sugar, and salt in a bowl.
2. Cut in butter until the mixture resembles coarse crumbs.
3. Add the egg and mix, then gradually add ice water until the dough forms.
4. Shape into a disc, wrap, and chill before rolling out.

Troubleshooting Pie Crust Issues

1. Crust Is Too Tough

  - Cause: Overmixing or overkneading the dough.
  - Solution: Handle the dough gently and chill it to relax gluten.

2. Crust Shrinks During Baking

  - Cause: Overworking the dough or insufficient chilling.

- Solution: Chill thoroughly and avoid stretching the dough when transferring it to the pie dish.

3. Soggy Bottom

- Cause: Filling too wet or crust underbaked.

- Solution: Use a metal pie dish and pre-bake the crust when needed.

Conclusion

Mastering the art of the perfect pie crust is a rewarding skill that elevates every pie you bake. Whether you're preparing a buttery, flaky crust for a fruit pie or a tender, savory base for a quiche, the techniques and recipes in this chapter provide a solid foundation. With practice and patience, you'll achieve crusts that are as beautiful as they are delicious—ready to complement any filling you dream up in the chapters ahead.

Chapter 2: Sweet vs. Savory Crusts

When crafting the perfect pie, the crust is more than just a vessel for the filling—it's an integral part of the flavor experience. Whether you're preparing a sweet, fruit-filled pie or a savory quiche, the crust must complement the filling to create a harmonious dish. Understanding how to adjust crust recipes for different types of pies allows you to elevate your creations from good to unforgettable.

This chapter explores the nuances of sweet and savory pie crusts, teaching you how to tailor your crust to suit the flavors of your pie. We'll cover the essential ingredients, techniques, and recipes for iconic crusts, including the graham cracker crust, chocolate cookie crust, and herbed pastry crust. By the end of this chapter, you'll be equipped to confidently craft crusts that perfectly pair with any filling.

The Role of the Crust in Sweet and Savory Pies

1. Balancing Flavors

The crust provides a counterpoint to the filling's flavor. A rich, buttery crust can mellow a tart lemon pie, while a lightly salted, herbed crust can enhance a savory chicken pot pie.

2. Texture Contrast

A well-made crust offers textural contrast: crisp and flaky for tender fillings or crumbly and firm for creamy or liquid-heavy pies.

3. Structural Support

The crust must be sturdy enough to hold the filling but tender enough to cut through easily without crumbling or becoming chewy.

4. Visual Appeal

The crust is the first thing people see when presented with a pie. Decorative edges, lattices, and even the color of the crust can make a strong impression.

Adjusting Crust Recipes for Sweet and Savory Pies

1. Sweet Crusts

Sweet crusts are typically used for dessert pies. The addition of sugar or other sweeteners enhances the crust's flavor and balances tart or tangy fillings.

Key Adjustments:

- Sugar: Adds sweetness and helps with browning. Use granulated or powdered sugar for subtle sweetness.

- Spices: Cinnamon, nutmeg, or vanilla extract can add depth to the flavor.

- Binders: Egg yolks or cream enrich the dough for a tender texture.

2. Savory Crusts

Savory crusts are tailored to pair with fillings like meats, cheeses, and vegetables. They are typically less rich and sweet, with added seasonings to enhance the savory flavors.

Key Adjustments:

- Salt: A higher salt content enhances savory flavors.

- Herbs and Spices: Rosemary, thyme, black pepper, or paprika can be incorporated directly into the dough.

- Cheese: Grated Parmesan or sharp cheddar can add a savory twist.

Techniques for Crafting Sweet and Savory Crusts

1. Cutting in the Fat

- For a flaky crust, use cold butter or shortening and leave pea-sized pieces of fat in the dough.

- For a crumbly crust, work the fat fully into the flour until the mixture resembles coarse sand.

2. Hydration

- Sweet crusts may use milk or cream for added richness.

- Savory crusts often benefit from the simplicity of ice water, but stock or wine can be used for added depth.

3. Chilling

Always chill the dough before rolling. This prevents the fat from melting prematurely and helps the crust hold its shape during baking.

4. Blind Baking

- For both sweet and savory pies with liquid-heavy fillings, blind baking ensures the crust doesn't become soggy.

- Line the crust with parchment paper, fill with weights, and bake at 375°F for 15-20 minutes.

Sweet Crust Recipes

1. Graham Cracker Crust

The graham cracker crust is a classic choice for cheesecakes, key lime pies, and other no-bake desserts.

Ingredients:

- 1 1/2 cups graham cracker crumbs
- 1/4 cup granulated sugar
- 6 tablespoons unsalted butter, melted

Instructions:

1. Prepare the Crumbs: Crush graham crackers into fine crumbs using a food processor or by placing them in a sealed bag and rolling over them with a rolling pin.

2. Combine Ingredients: In a bowl, mix graham cracker crumbs, sugar, and melted butter until evenly moistened.

3. Press into Pan: Press the mixture firmly into the bottom and up the sides of a pie dish. Use the back of a spoon or a measuring cup to compact the crust.

4. Bake or Chill:

- For baked pies: Preheat oven to 350°F and bake the crust for 8-10 minutes. Let cool before adding filling.

- For no-bake pies: Chill the crust in the refrigerator for at least 30 minutes before adding the filling.

Pro Tip: Add a pinch of cinnamon or nutmeg for an extra layer of flavor.

2. Chocolate Cookie Crust

Rich and indulgent, this crust is perfect for chocolate mousse pies or peanut butter pies.

Ingredients:

- 1 1/2 cups chocolate wafer cookie crumbs

- 1/4 cup granulated sugar

- 6 tablespoons unsalted butter, melted

Instructions:

1. Prepare the Crumbs: Crush chocolate wafer cookies into fine crumbs.

2. Mix Ingredients: Combine cookie crumbs, sugar, and melted butter in a bowl. Stir until evenly combined.

3. Press into Pan: Press the mixture into a pie dish, ensuring an even layer on the bottom and sides.

4. Bake or Chill:

- For baked pies: Bake at 350°F for 8-10 minutes. Let cool before adding filling.

- For no-bake pies: Chill for at least 30 minutes before filling.

Pro Tip: Substitute crushed Oreo cookies for an extra-rich crust.

Savory Crust Recipe

Herbed Pastry Crust

This versatile crust pairs beautifully with quiches, savory tarts, and pot pies.

Ingredients:

- 2 1/2 cups all-purpose flour

- 1 teaspoon salt

- 1 teaspoon dried thyme or rosemary, finely chopped

- 1/4 cup grated Parmesan cheese (optional)

- 1 cup (2 sticks) unsalted butter, cold and cubed

- 6-8 tablespoons ice water

Instructions:

1. Combine Dry Ingredients: In a large bowl, whisk together flour, salt, herbs, and Parmesan (if using).

2. Cut in the Butter: Add cold butter and cut into the flour until the mixture resembles coarse crumbs.

3. Add Water: Gradually add ice water, 1 tablespoon at a time, mixing until the dough just comes together.

4. Chill: Divide the dough in half, shape into discs, and wrap in plastic wrap. Chill for at least 30 minutes.

5. Roll Out and Bake: Roll out the dough on a floured surface and use as needed for your savory pie. Blind bake if required.

Pro Tip: For an extra savory punch, brush the crust with an egg wash and sprinkle with flaky sea salt before baking.

Pairing Sweet and Savory Crusts with Fillings

Sweet Crust Pairings

- Graham Cracker Crust: Cheesecakes, key lime pies, and frozen desserts.
- Chocolate Cookie Crust: Chocolate mousse pies, peanut butter pies, and ice cream pies.

Savory Crust Pairings

- Herbed Pastry Crust: Chicken pot pies, vegetable quiches, and meat tarts.

Conclusion

Crafting the right crust for your pie is an essential step in pie-making. By understanding the differences between sweet and savory crusts and learning how to adjust recipes accordingly, you can elevate the flavor and texture of your pies. Whether you're crushing graham crackers for a silky cheesecake or folding rosemary into a buttery dough for a quiche, the crust becomes a defining element that enhances every bite. In the next chapter, we'll explore the tools and techniques that will make your pie-making journey even smoother. Let's keep baking!

Chapter 3: Pie-Making Tools and Techniques

A beautifully crafted pie is as much about skill as it is about the tools you use. From achieving a flaky crust to creating intricate latticework, the right tools and techniques are essential for pie-making success. This chapter delves into the must-have tools every pie maker should own and the techniques that transform a simple pie into a stunning masterpiece.

We'll explore the key tools that make pie-making easier, techniques for decorative edges and latticework, and tips for achieving the perfect golden crust. By mastering these tools and techniques, you'll elevate your pies from basic to bakery-quality, impressing family and friends with every creation.

Essential Tools for Pie-Making

1. Rolling Pins

A good rolling pin is the foundation of a well-rolled crust. The type of rolling pin you choose depends on your comfort and pie-making style.

Types of Rolling Pins

- Classic Wooden Rolling Pin: A traditional option with handles that provide control. Ideal for beginners.
    - French Rolling Pin: Tapered at the ends, allowing for greater control and maneuverability. Perfect for delicate doughs.
    - Marble Rolling Pin: Heavy and smooth, great for rolling out chilled dough without warming it.
    - Non-Stick Rolling Pin: Coated to prevent sticking, making it useful for working with sticky doughs or humid environments.
    Pro Tip: Lightly flour your rolling pin before use to prevent sticking, but avoid over-flouring, which can make the dough tough.

2. Pastry Mat or Countertop Cover

A pastry mat provides a non-stick surface for rolling out dough, with measurements and guidelines to help achieve the perfect size and shape.

3. Pie Dish

The choice of pie dish affects how your pie bakes and its presentation.

Types of Pie Dishes

- Glass: Allows you to see if the crust is browning evenly. Great for custard pies and quiches.
    - Metal: Conducts heat quickly, resulting in crispier crusts. Ideal for double-crust pies.
    - Ceramic: Retains heat for even baking, with beautiful designs perfect for serving.

4. Pie Weights

Pie weights are crucial for blind baking, preventing the crust from puffing up or shrinking during pre-baking.
    - Options include ceramic weights, dried beans, or even rice.

5. Pastry Cutter or Blender

Used to cut fat (butter, shortening, or lard) into flour, creating the coarse crumbs needed for a flaky crust.

6. Pastry Brush

Essential for applying egg wash, melted butter, or milk to achieve a golden crust.

7. Crimping Tools

Crimping tools or even simple forks help create decorative edges that give your pie a polished, professional look.

8. Bench Scraper

A versatile tool for gathering and transferring dough, cutting portions, or scraping your work surface clean.

9. Lattice Cutter or Pastry Wheel

A lattice cutter creates uniform strips for decorative latticework, while a pastry wheel can add fluted edges to your dough strips.

10. Paring Knife and Kitchen Scissors

Used for trimming excess dough, scoring designs, and cutting vents into the top crust.

Pie-Making Techniques

1. Rolling Out Dough

Properly rolled dough ensures an even crust that bakes beautifully and holds the filling without breaking.

Steps for Rolling Dough:

1. Prepare Your Surface: Lightly flour your work surface and rolling pin.

2. Start from the Center: Roll from the center outward, rotating the dough slightly after each roll to maintain a circular shape.

3. Check for Size: Roll the dough to about 1/8-inch thick and ensure it's at least 2 inches larger than your pie dish.

4. Transfer the Dough: Gently roll the dough onto your rolling pin or fold it into quarters to lift and place it in the pie dish.

2. Blind Baking

Blind baking is essential for pies with fillings that don't require baking, like cream pies, or when you need a partially baked crust for wetter fillings.

Steps for Blind Baking:

1. Line the unbaked crust with parchment paper or foil.

2. Fill with pie weights, beans, or rice to prevent puffing.

3. Bake at 375°F for 15-20 minutes.

4. Remove the weights and parchment, then bake for another 5-10 minutes until lightly golden.

3. Crimping and Decorative Edges

The edge of a pie crust isn't just functional—it's a chance to add artistry to your pie.

Techniques for Crimping:

- Fork Crimp: Press the tines of a fork along the edge for a simple, classic design.

- Pinch and Flute: Use your thumb and forefinger on one hand and a knuckle on the other to create a wavy edge.

- Braided Edge: Roll thin strips of dough and braid them together, attaching them to the pie's edge with egg wash.

4. Latticework

A lattice crust is both beautiful and functional, allowing steam to escape from fruit-filled pies while showcasing the filling.

Steps for Latticework:

1. Roll out the top crust and cut it into strips (about 1/2 inch wide).

2. Lay half the strips horizontally across the pie.

3. Weave the remaining strips vertically, lifting alternating horizontal strips to create a woven pattern.

4. Trim and crimp the edges to secure the lattice.

Pro Tip: Use a pastry wheel for fluted edges on your lattice strips.

5. Scoring and Venting

For closed-top pies, scoring or cutting vents is necessary to allow steam to escape and prevent sogginess.

Techniques:

- Simple Slits: Use a sharp knife to cut evenly spaced slits in the dough.
   - Decorative Shapes: Use small cookie cutters to create designs in the top crust.
   - Lattice Alternative: Overlap dough cutouts (e.g., leaves, hearts) for a unique design.

Achieving the Perfect Golden Crust

The hallmark of a well-made pie is a golden, evenly baked crust. Here's how to achieve it every time:

1. Egg Wash
   An egg wash gives the crust a shiny, golden finish. Mix one egg with a tablespoon of water or milk and brush it lightly over the crust before baking.
   2. Alternative Washes
   - Milk or Cream: Creates a matte finish and enhances browning.
   - Sugar Sprinkles: For sweet pies, sprinkle coarse sugar over the wash for added texture and shine.
   3. Even Baking
   - Use the middle rack for uniform heat distribution.
   - Rotate the pie halfway through baking to ensure even browning.
   4. Foil or Shield
   If the edges brown too quickly, cover them with foil or a pie crust shield to prevent burning.

Common Mistakes and How to Avoid Them

1. Soggy Bottom Crust
   - Cause: Insufficient blind baking or too much moisture in the filling.
   - Solution: Blind bake the crust and use a metal pie dish for better heat conduction.

2. Over-Browned Crust
   - Cause: High oven temperature or prolonged baking.
   - Solution: Use a pie shield or cover the edges with foil once they've browned.
   3. Cracking Dough
   - Cause: Dough was too dry or over-chilled.
   - Solution: Let the dough rest at room temperature for 10 minutes before rolling.

Conclusion

The tools and techniques discussed in this chapter are the foundation for crafting pies that not only taste amazing but also look professional. From mastering decorative edges and latticework to ensuring a golden, flaky crust, these skills will take your pie-making to new heights. Armed with the right tools and an understanding of essential techniques, you're ready to create show-stopping pies that will delight both the eyes and the palate. In the next chapter, we'll dive into the world of sweet pies, exploring classic recipes that showcase these newfound skills. Let's roll out that dough and get baking!

Chapter 4: Fruit Pies for Every Season

Fruit pies are the epitome of classic desserts, celebrated for their ability to capture the essence of every season. From the warm, spiced apple pies of fall to the bright, juicy peach pies of summer, fruit pies offer endless possibilities for showcasing seasonal produce. This chapter will guide you through the art of crafting perfect fruit pies, featuring recipes for apple, cherry, and peach pies. You'll also learn how to balance sweetness and acidity in fruit fillings, work with fresh, frozen, or canned fruits, and create pies that celebrate the best flavors of each season.

The Basics of Fruit Pies

1. The Role of Fruit

Fruit is the star of any fruit pie, and its natural sweetness and acidity form the foundation of the filling. Selecting the right fruit and understanding its properties are crucial for creating a balanced pie.

2. Sweetness and Acidity

Balancing sweetness and acidity is essential for a flavorful filling. While some fruits, like peaches, are naturally sweet, others, like cherries, may require more sugar to offset their tartness. Conversely, overly sweet fruits can benefit from a touch of lemon juice or other acidic ingredients to brighten their flavor.

3. Thickening Agents

Fruit fillings release juices during baking, and thickening agents are used to achieve the perfect consistency. Common options include:

- Cornstarch: Creates a clear, glossy filling.

- Flour: Yields a more opaque filling.

- Tapioca Starch: Excellent for thickening without altering the flavor.

4. Working with Different Types of Fruit

- Fresh Fruit: Offers the best flavor and texture but may require additional preparation, like peeling or slicing.

- Frozen Fruit: Convenient and available year-round, though it may release more liquid during baking.

- Canned Fruit: Pre-cooked and ready to use, but often sweeter due to added syrups.

Seasonal Fruit Pie Recipes

1. Classic Apple Pie

Apple pie is a quintessential dessert that combines sweet, tender apples with a flaky, buttery crust. Perfect for autumn, it's a timeless favorite at family gatherings and holidays.

Ingredients (Serves 8):

For the Crust:

- 2 1/2 cups all-purpose flour

- 1 teaspoon salt

- 1 teaspoon sugar

- 1 cup (2 sticks) unsalted butter, cold and cubed

- 6-8 tablespoons ice water

For the Filling:

- 6-8 medium apples (Granny Smith, Honeycrisp, or a mix), peeled, cored, and sliced

- 3/4 cup granulated sugar

- 1/4 cup brown sugar

- 2 tablespoons all-purpose flour

- 1 tablespoon cornstarch

- 1 teaspoon ground cinnamon

- 1/4 teaspoon ground nutmeg

- 1 tablespoon lemon juice

- 2 tablespoons unsalted butter, cubed

Instructions:

1. Prepare the Crust:

- Combine flour, salt, and sugar in a bowl. Cut in butter until the mixture resembles coarse crumbs. Gradually add ice water, mixing until the dough just comes together. Divide into two discs, wrap in plastic, and chill for at least 30 minutes.

2. Make the Filling:

- In a large bowl, toss the apple slices with sugars, flour, cornstarch, cinnamon, nutmeg, and lemon juice. Let sit for 15 minutes to release juices.

3. Assemble the Pie:

- Roll out one dough disc and line a 9-inch pie dish. Add the apple filling and dot with butter. Roll out the second disc and place it over the filling. Trim and crimp the edges, and cut slits in the top for venting.

4. Bake:

- Preheat oven to 375°F. Bake the pie for 50-60 minutes, covering the edges with foil if they brown too quickly. Let cool before serving.

Pro Tip: For a glossy finish, brush the top crust with an egg wash and sprinkle with coarse sugar before baking.

2. Sweet Cherry Pie

Cherry pie is a summer classic that showcases the sweet-tart flavor of ripe cherries. Whether using fresh or frozen cherries, this recipe captures the season's essence.

Ingredients (Serves 8):

For the Crust:

- Same as Apple Pie crust recipe.

For the Filling:

- 4 cups pitted cherries (sweet or sour, fresh or frozen)

- 1 cup granulated sugar (adjust based on the cherries' tartness)

- 1/4 cup cornstarch

- 1 tablespoon lemon juice

- 1 teaspoon vanilla extract

- 1 tablespoon unsalted butter, cubed

Instructions:

1. Prepare the Crust:

- Follow the crust preparation steps from the apple pie recipe.

2. Make the Filling:

- In a large bowl, combine cherries, sugar, cornstarch, lemon juice, and vanilla extract. Toss to coat evenly.

3. Assemble the Pie:

- Roll out the first dough disc and line a 9-inch pie dish. Pour in the cherry filling and dot with butter. Roll out the second disc, cut into strips, and create a lattice top. Trim and crimp the edges.

4. Bake:

- Preheat oven to 400°F. Bake the pie for 40-50 minutes, reducing the temperature to 375°F halfway through. Let cool completely before slicing.

Pro Tip: Use a mix of sweet and sour cherries for a balanced flavor profile.

3. Juicy Peach Pie

Peach pie is a summer delight, featuring sweet, juicy peaches in a flaky crust. This recipe is simple yet bursting with flavor.

Ingredients (Serves 8):

For the Crust:

- Same as Apple Pie crust recipe.

For the Filling:

- 6-8 ripe peaches, peeled, pitted, and sliced
- 3/4 cup granulated sugar
- 2 tablespoons brown sugar
- 2 tablespoons cornstarch
- 1/4 teaspoon ground cinnamon
- 1/4 teaspoon ground ginger
- 1 tablespoon lemon juice
- 1 teaspoon vanilla extract
- 1 tablespoon unsalted butter, cubed

Instructions:

1. Prepare the Crust:

- Follow the crust preparation steps from the apple pie recipe.

2. Make the Filling:

- In a large bowl, toss peach slices with sugars, cornstarch, cinnamon, ginger, lemon juice, and vanilla extract. Let sit for 10 minutes.

3. Assemble the Pie:

- Roll out the first dough disc and line a 9-inch pie dish. Add the peach filling and dot with butter. Roll out the second disc, cut into shapes (e.g., hearts or stars), and place on top of the filling. Trim and crimp the edges.

4. Bake:

- Preheat oven to 375°F. Bake the pie for 45-55 minutes, covering the edges if necessary. Cool for at least 2 hours before serving.

Pro Tip: Brush the top crust with a mixture of cream and sugar for a caramelized finish.

Tips for Perfect Fruit Pies

1. Balancing Sweetness and Acidity
   - Add lemon juice or zest to overly sweet fruits for brightness.
   - Adjust sugar levels based on the natural sweetness of the fruit.
2. Handling Juicy Fruits
- Toss fruit with sugar and let sit to draw out excess juice, then drain or thicken with cornstarch.
   - Pre-cook filling slightly to control moisture and prevent soggy crusts.
3. Working with Different Types of Fruit
- Fresh: Choose ripe, in-season fruit for the best flavor.
- Frozen: Thaw and drain excess liquid before use.
- Canned: Rinse off syrup to control sweetness and reduce added sugar in the recipe.

Conclusion

Fruit pies are a celebration of nature's bounty, capturing the essence of every season in a flaky, buttery crust. Whether you're savoring the spiced warmth of an apple pie, the tangy sweetness of a cherry pie, or the juicy brightness of a peach pie, these recipes offer something for every occasion. By mastering the tips and techniques in this chapter, you'll be able to craft fruit pies that delight the senses and showcase the best of each season. Let the pie-making adventure continue in the next chapter, where we explore creamy and custard pies!

Chapter 5: Creamy and Custard Pies

Creamy and custard pies occupy a special place in the world of desserts. Their silky textures and rich flavors are both comforting and indulgent. From the tropical sweetness of coconut cream pie to the nostalgic charm of banana cream pie and the tangy simplicity of buttermilk pie, these desserts showcase the magic of combining eggs, cream, and sugar into velvety perfection.

In this chapter, we'll explore the techniques and tips necessary to create flawless creamy and custard pies. We'll also provide step-by-step recipes for coconut cream pie, banana cream pie, and buttermilk pie, along with essential guidance on stabilizing whipped cream toppings to ensure your pies look as stunning as they taste.

The Basics of Creamy and Custard Pies

1. What Are Creamy and Custard Pies?

- Creamy Pies: These pies typically feature a pre-baked crust filled with a smooth, chilled mixture made from dairy, eggs, and flavorings. Examples include coconut cream pie and banana cream pie.

- Custard Pies: Custard pies, like buttermilk pie, are baked with a liquid filling made from eggs, milk or cream, and sugar, which sets into a firm, sliceable texture.

2. The Importance of Texture

The hallmark of creamy and custard pies is their silky texture. Achieving this requires careful attention to ingredients, mixing techniques, and cooking times.

3. Balancing Flavors

While these pies are often rich and indulgent, they require balance to avoid overwhelming sweetness. Adding acidity, such as lemon juice or buttermilk, enhances flavor and creates a more complex dessert.

Techniques for Silky Smooth Fillings

1. Proper Mixing

- Creamy Pies: Whisk your ingredients thoroughly but gently to avoid over-incorporating air, which can lead to bubbles or cracks.

- Custard Pies: Combine ingredients until just smooth; overmixing can cause the filling to puff up during baking and collapse when cooled.

2. Cooking Techniques

- Stovetop Fillings: Many creamy pies require cooking the filling on the stovetop. Use medium heat and stir constantly to prevent lumps or scorching.

- Baked Fillings: For custards, bake at a moderate temperature (325°F–350°F) to ensure even cooking without curdling.

3. Straining

For the smoothest texture, strain your filling through a fine-mesh sieve to remove any lumps or bits of curdled egg.

4. Preventing Cracks

- Avoid overbaking custard pies, as this can cause the filling to crack. The filling should jiggle slightly in the center when removed from the oven.

- Bake custards in a water bath to regulate temperature and prevent overheating.

5. Cooling and Chilling

- Allow pies to cool to room temperature before chilling in the refrigerator. This gradual cooling process prevents condensation and ensures the filling sets properly.

Recipes

1. Coconut Cream Pie

A tropical delight, coconut cream pie combines a flaky crust with a luscious coconut custard filling, topped with whipped cream and toasted coconut flakes.

Ingredients (Serves 8):

For the Crust:

- 1 pre-baked pie crust (use your favorite recipe or a store-bought crust)

For the Filling:

- 1 cup whole milk

- 1 cup coconut milk (canned)
- 1/2 cup granulated sugar
- 1/4 cup cornstarch
- 4 large egg yolks
- 1/4 teaspoon salt
- 1 teaspoon vanilla extract
- 1 cup sweetened shredded coconut
For the Topping:
- 1 cup heavy cream
- 2 tablespoons powdered sugar
- 1/2 teaspoon vanilla extract
- 1/4 cup toasted coconut flakes
Instructions:
1. Prepare the Filling:
- In a medium saucepan, combine milk, coconut milk, sugar, and salt. Heat over medium heat until steaming (but not boiling).
- In a separate bowl, whisk egg yolks and cornstarch until smooth. Slowly pour about 1/2 cup of the hot milk mixture into the yolks, whisking constantly to temper them.
- Return the tempered mixture to the saucepan and cook, stirring constantly, until thickened (about 2–3 minutes). Remove from heat and stir in vanilla extract and shredded coconut.
2. Assemble the Pie:
- Pour the filling into the pre-baked crust and smooth the top. Cover with plastic wrap, pressing it directly onto the surface to prevent a skin from forming. Chill for at least 4 hours.
3. Make the Whipped Topping:
- Beat heavy cream, powdered sugar, and vanilla extract until stiff peaks form. Spread over the chilled filling and garnish with toasted coconut flakes.

2. Banana Cream Pie

Banana cream pie layers ripe bananas with a silky vanilla custard and fluffy whipped cream, creating a nostalgic favorite.
Ingredients (Serves 8):

For the Crust:
- 1 pre-baked graham cracker crust (store-bought or homemade)
For the Filling:
- 2 cups whole milk
- 1/2 cup granulated sugar
- 1/4 cup cornstarch
- 4 large egg yolks
- 1/4 teaspoon salt
- 1 teaspoon vanilla extract
- 2 tablespoons unsalted butter
- 3 ripe bananas, sliced
For the Topping:
- 1 cup heavy cream
- 2 tablespoons powdered sugar
- 1/2 teaspoon vanilla extract
Instructions:
1. Prepare the Filling:
- In a medium saucepan, heat milk and sugar over medium heat until steaming.
- In a separate bowl, whisk cornstarch, egg yolks, and salt until smooth. Gradually whisk in 1/2 cup of the hot milk mixture to temper the yolks.
- Return the mixture to the saucepan and cook, stirring constantly, until thickened. Remove from heat and stir in vanilla extract and butter.
2. Layer the Pie:
- Arrange banana slices in the bottom of the graham cracker crust. Pour the custard over the bananas and smooth the top. Cover with plastic wrap and chill for at least 4 hours.
3. Top and Serve:
- Whip the heavy cream, powdered sugar, and vanilla extract until stiff peaks form. Spread over the pie and garnish with additional banana slices, if desired.

3. Buttermilk Pie

Buttermilk pie is a Southern classic, featuring a tangy, creamy custard filling baked in a buttery crust.

Ingredients (Serves 8):

For the Crust:

- 1 unbaked pie crust (use your favorite recipe)

For the Filling:

- 1 1/2 cups granulated sugar

- 1/4 cup unsalted butter, melted

- 3 large eggs

- 3 tablespoons all-purpose flour

- 1 cup buttermilk

- 1 teaspoon vanilla extract

- 1/4 teaspoon nutmeg (optional)

Instructions:

1. Prepare the Filling:

- Preheat oven to 350°F.

- In a large bowl, whisk together sugar, melted butter, and eggs until smooth. Add flour, buttermilk, vanilla extract, and nutmeg, whisking until well combined.

2. Assemble the Pie:

- Pour the filling into the unbaked pie crust.

3. Bake:

- Bake for 45–55 minutes, or until the filling is set and lightly golden. Let cool to room temperature before slicing.

Tips for Stabilizing Whipped Cream Toppings

Whipped cream toppings are essential for creamy pies but can deflate or weep if not handled properly. Here are tips for ensuring your whipped cream stays picture-perfect:

1. Use Cold Equipment

- Chill your mixing bowl and beaters before whipping cream to achieve better volume and stability.

2. Add Stabilizers

- Powdered Sugar: Contains cornstarch, which helps stabilize the cream.

- Gelatin: Dissolve 1 teaspoon gelatin in 2 tablespoons warm water, then mix into whipped cream.

3. Whip to Stiff Peaks

- Beat the cream until stiff peaks form, but avoid overwhipping, which can turn it grainy.

4. Apply Just Before Serving

- For the freshest presentation, add whipped cream topping shortly before serving.

Conclusion

Creamy and custard pies are a testament to the art of creating smooth, luscious desserts. Whether you're crafting a tropical coconut cream pie, a nostalgic banana cream pie, or a tangy buttermilk pie, the techniques and tips in this chapter will ensure your pies are as beautiful as they are delicious. With perfectly stabilized whipped cream toppings and silky fillings, you'll impress everyone who takes a bite. Let's continue our pie journey in the next chapter with chocolate and nut-filled decadence!

Chapter 6: Decadent Chocolate Pies

Chocolate pies are the epitome of indulgence, combining rich, velvety textures with deep, complex flavors. These pies are a dream for chocolate lovers, offering a variety of forms—from creamy French silk to airy chocolate mousse and nostalgic s'mores pies. Each type highlights the versatility of chocolate, showcasing its ability to elevate desserts to extraordinary heights.

In this chapter, we'll explore how to work with different types of chocolate, share detailed recipes for three decadent chocolate pies, and provide guidance on pairing chocolate with complementary flavors. By mastering these techniques and recipes, you'll be equipped to create chocolate pies that impress every time.

Understanding Chocolate in Pies

1. Types of Chocolate

Using the right type of chocolate is key to achieving the desired flavor and texture in your pie.

a. Dark Chocolate

- Contains a high percentage of cocoa solids, offering a rich, slightly bitter flavor.

- Best for pies with intense chocolate flavors, like French silk pie.

b. Milk Chocolate

- Creamy and sweet, with a lower cocoa percentage and higher milk content.

- Ideal for lighter, sweeter pies like chocolate mousse.

c. White Chocolate

- Made from cocoa butter, sugar, and milk solids, without cocoa solids.

- Adds a creamy, subtle sweetness to pies.

d. Semi-Sweet and Bittersweet Chocolate

- Common in baking, these chocolates strike a balance between sweetness and intensity.

- Versatile for most chocolate pie recipes.

2. Melting Chocolate

Properly melted chocolate ensures smooth, luscious fillings. Here are some tips:

- Double Boiler Method: Place chocolate in a heatproof bowl over a pot of simmering water, stirring until melted.

- Microwave Method: Heat chocolate in short bursts (20–30 seconds) and stir between each interval to prevent scorching.

3. Enhancing Chocolate Flavor

- Salt: A pinch of salt enhances chocolate's natural flavors.

- Coffee or Espresso Powder: Adds depth and intensity to chocolate desserts.

- Alcohol: Liqueurs like Kahlúa, Grand Marnier, or bourbon complement chocolate beautifully.

Recipes

1. French Silk Pie

French silk pie is a classic, featuring a buttery crust filled with smooth, chocolatey custard and topped with whipped cream.

Ingredients (Serves 8):

For the Crust:

- 1 pre-baked pie crust (use your favorite recipe or a store-bought crust)

For the Filling:

- 4 ounces bittersweet chocolate, melted and cooled

- 1 cup unsalted butter, softened

- 1 1/4 cups granulated sugar

- 4 large eggs (pasteurized)

- 2 teaspoons vanilla extract

For the Topping:
- 1 cup heavy cream
- 2 tablespoons powdered sugar
- Chocolate shavings (for garnish)

Instructions:

1. Prepare the Crust:
- Ensure your crust is pre-baked and cooled before filling.

2. Make the Filling:
- In a large bowl, beat butter and sugar until light and fluffy (about 3 minutes).
- Gradually add melted chocolate and vanilla extract, mixing until smooth.
- Add eggs one at a time, beating for 3 minutes after each addition to ensure a light, airy texture.

3. Assemble the Pie:
- Pour the filling into the pre-baked crust and smooth the top. Chill for at least 4 hours, or until set.

4. Prepare the Topping:
- Whip heavy cream and powdered sugar until stiff peaks form. Spread or pipe over the chilled filling. Garnish with chocolate shavings.

Pro Tip: For an extra layer of flavor, brush the crust with a thin layer of melted chocolate before adding the filling.

2. Chocolate Mousse Pie

Light and airy, chocolate mousse pie combines the richness of chocolate with a cloud-like texture.

Ingredients (Serves 8):

For the Crust:
- 1 pre-baked chocolate cookie crust (use crushed Oreo cookies or store-bought)

For the Filling:
- 6 ounces semi-sweet chocolate, melted and cooled
- 3 large egg yolks

- 1/4 cup granulated sugar
- 1 1/2 cups heavy cream
- 1 teaspoon vanilla extract

For the Topping:

- 1 cup heavy cream
- 2 tablespoons powdered sugar
- Chocolate curls or cocoa powder (for garnish)

Instructions:

1. Prepare the Crust:

- Ensure the crust is pre-baked and cooled.

2. Make the Mousse Filling:

- In a medium bowl, whisk egg yolks and sugar until pale and creamy. Gradually whisk in melted chocolate and vanilla extract.

- In a separate bowl, whip heavy cream to soft peaks. Gently fold the whipped cream into the chocolate mixture in three additions until fully combined.

3. Assemble the Pie:

- Pour the mousse filling into the crust and smooth the top. Chill for at least 4 hours, or until set.

4. Add the Topping:

- Whip heavy cream and powdered sugar until stiff peaks form. Spread or pipe over the mousse. Garnish with chocolate curls or a dusting of cocoa powder.

Pro Tip: Add a splash of coffee liqueur or espresso powder to the mousse for a sophisticated flavor twist.

3. S'mores Pie

This nostalgic pie brings the flavors of campfire s'mores to your table, with layers of chocolate ganache, graham cracker crust, and toasted marshmallows.

Ingredients (Serves 8):

For the Crust:

- 1 1/2 cups graham cracker crumbs
- 1/4 cup granulated sugar
- 6 tablespoons unsalted butter, melted

For the Filling:
- 8 ounces semi-sweet chocolate, chopped
- 1 cup heavy cream
- 1 teaspoon vanilla extract
For the Topping:
- 2 cups mini marshmallows

Instructions:

1. Prepare the Crust:

- Preheat oven to 350°F. Mix graham cracker crumbs, sugar, and melted butter in a bowl. Press into a 9-inch pie dish. Bake for 8–10 minutes and let cool.

2. Make the Ganache Filling:

- Heat heavy cream in a saucepan until just steaming. Pour over chopped chocolate in a bowl and let sit for 2 minutes. Stir until smooth and glossy. Add vanilla extract.

3. Assemble the Pie:

- Pour the ganache into the cooled crust and smooth the top. Chill for 2–3 hours, or until firm.

4. Add the Marshmallow Topping:

- Preheat your broiler. Spread mini marshmallows evenly over the ganache. Place under the broiler for 1–2 minutes, watching closely, until marshmallows are golden and toasted.

Pro Tip: For an even toast, use a kitchen torch to brown the marshmallows.

Pairing Chocolate with Complementary Flavors

Chocolate's versatility allows it to pair beautifully with a wide range of flavors. Here are some classic combinations to inspire your pies:

1. Nuts
  - Almonds, hazelnuts, and pecans add crunch and enhance chocolate's richness.
  - Try a chocolate-hazelnut filling or sprinkle chopped nuts over whipped cream toppings.

2. Fruits
  - Berries: Raspberries, strawberries, and cherries provide a tart contrast to chocolate's sweetness.
  - Citrus: Orange zest or lime pairs wonderfully with dark or milk chocolate.
  3. Spices
  - Cinnamon, nutmeg, and chili powder bring warmth and depth to chocolate pies.
  - Add a pinch of cayenne for a spicy kick.
  4. Coffee and Alcohol
  - Espresso powder intensifies chocolate's flavor in pies like French silk.
  - Incorporate liqueurs like Baileys, Grand Marnier, or Amaretto for an elegant twist.

Tips for Perfect Chocolate Pies

1. Choose High-Quality Chocolate: Use good-quality chocolate with at least 60% cocoa for the best flavor and texture.
  2. Balance Sweetness: Adjust sugar levels based on the type of chocolate used to prevent overly sweet pies.
  3. Layer Textures: Combine creamy fillings with crunchy crusts or nut toppings for added interest.

Conclusion

Decadent chocolate pies are the ultimate indulgence, offering rich flavors and luxurious textures that captivate dessert lovers. Whether you're savoring the airy elegance of chocolate mousse pie, the nostalgia of a gooey s'mores pie, or the silky sophistication of French silk pie, these recipes are sure to impress. By mastering the techniques and pairing chocolate with complementary flavors, you'll elevate your chocolate pies to works of art. Let's continue our pie-making journey in the next chapter with nut and caramel-infused delights!

Chapter 7: Holiday Favorites

Holiday pies are more than just desserts—they're traditions, family memories, and celebrations all wrapped into a flaky crust. From the warmth of pumpkin pie at Thanksgiving to the nutty sweetness of pecan pie and the spiced decadence of mincemeat pie, these festive treats are an essential part of any holiday table.

This chapter will guide you through crafting these holiday classics, explore the spices and flavor profiles that define them, and provide inspiration for creative holiday-themed decorations to make your pies the centerpiece of your celebrations.

The Role of Pies in Holiday Celebrations

Pies have long been a staple of holiday gatherings. Their versatility and ability to highlight seasonal ingredients make them ideal for festive occasions. Each pie tells a story and evokes the flavors of its season—pumpkin pie brings warm spices to chilly autumn evenings, while pecan pie offers a rich, nutty sweetness perfect for winter holidays.

1. Tradition and Nostalgia

- Pies are steeped in tradition, often passed down through generations.

- Baking pies together becomes a cherished holiday ritual, connecting families through shared recipes and stories.

2. Seasonal Ingredients

- Holiday pies emphasize the bounty of the season: pumpkins, nuts, dried fruits, and warm spices.

- These ingredients create desserts that are as comforting as they are celebratory.

3. A Show-Stopping Centerpiece

- With creative decorations and thoughtful presentation, holiday pies can double as edible art, enhancing your holiday table.

Recipes

1. Classic Pumpkin Pie

Pumpkin pie is synonymous with Thanksgiving, offering a creamy, spiced filling nestled in a flaky crust.

Ingredients (Serves 8):

For the Crust:

- 1 unbaked pie crust (use your favorite recipe or store-bought)

For the Filling:

- 1 can (15 ounces) pumpkin puree
- 3/4 cup granulated sugar
- 1/4 cup brown sugar
- 2 large eggs
- 1 egg yolk
- 1 1/2 teaspoons ground cinnamon
- 1/2 teaspoon ground ginger
- 1/4 teaspoon ground nutmeg
- 1/4 teaspoon ground cloves
- 1/2 teaspoon salt
- 1 cup heavy cream
- 1/4 cup whole milk
- 1 teaspoon vanilla extract

Instructions:

1. Prepare the Crust:

- Roll out the dough and fit it into a 9-inch pie dish. Trim and crimp the edges. Chill the crust for 30 minutes.

2. Make the Filling:

- In a large bowl, whisk together pumpkin puree, sugars, eggs, yolk, spices, and salt. Stir in cream, milk, and vanilla extract until smooth.

3. Assemble and Bake:

- Pour the filling into the prepared crust. Preheat oven to 425°F and bake for 15 minutes. Reduce the temperature to 350°F and bake for an additional 40–50 minutes, or until the filling is set but slightly jiggly in the center.

4. Cool and Serve:

- Cool to room temperature before serving with whipped cream or a dollop of crème fraîche.

Pro Tip: For a decorative touch, use pie crust scraps to cut out leaf or pumpkin shapes, bake them separately, and place them on top of the cooled pie.

2. Pecan Pie

Pecan pie is a rich and indulgent dessert, featuring a gooey, buttery filling studded with crunchy pecans.

Ingredients (Serves 8):

For the Crust:

- 1 unbaked pie crust (use your favorite recipe or store-bought)

For the Filling:

- 1 cup light corn syrup

- 1 cup granulated sugar

- 1/2 cup unsalted butter, melted

- 3 large eggs

- 1 teaspoon vanilla extract

- 1/4 teaspoon salt

- 1 1/2 cups pecan halves

Instructions:

1. Prepare the Crust:

- Roll out the dough and fit it into a 9-inch pie dish. Trim and crimp the edges.

2. Make the Filling:

- In a large bowl, whisk together corn syrup, sugar, melted butter, eggs, vanilla, and salt until smooth. Stir in pecans.

3. Assemble and Bake:

- Pour the filling into the prepared crust. Preheat oven to 350°F and bake for 50–60 minutes, or until the filling is set and slightly puffed. Cover the edges with foil if they brown too quickly.

4. Cool and Serve:

- Cool completely before slicing to allow the filling to set. Serve with whipped cream or a drizzle of caramel sauce.

Pro Tip: Arrange pecan halves in a decorative pattern on top of the filling before baking for an elegant presentation.

3. Mincemeat Pie

Mincemeat pie is a festive, spiced dessert filled with a mixture of dried fruits, spices, and sometimes a splash of brandy or rum.

Ingredients (Serves 8):

For the Crust:

- 1 double pie crust (use your favorite recipe or store-bought)

For the Filling:

- 2 cups prepared mincemeat (homemade or store-bought)
- 1/2 cup diced apple
- 1/4 cup brown sugar
- 1/4 teaspoon ground cinnamon
- 1/8 teaspoon ground cloves
- 2 tablespoons brandy or rum (optional)

Instructions:

1. Prepare the Filling:

- In a bowl, mix mincemeat, apple, brown sugar, cinnamon, cloves, and brandy or rum.

2. Assemble the Pie:

- Roll out one crust and line a 9-inch pie dish. Fill with the mincemeat mixture. Roll out the second crust and place it over the filling, trimming and crimping the edges. Cut slits for venting.

3. Bake:

- Preheat oven to 375°F and bake for 40–50 minutes, or until the crust is golden brown.

4. Cool and Serve:

- Cool slightly before serving warm with vanilla ice cream or custard.

Pro Tip: Use a lattice top or cut festive shapes into the top crust for added holiday flair.

Spices and Flavor Profiles for Festive Pies

1. Warm Spices

The hallmark of holiday pies is the use of warm spices, which evoke a sense of comfort and celebration.

- Cinnamon: Adds sweetness and warmth.
- Nutmeg: Earthy and slightly sweet, perfect for custards and creams.
- Ginger: Spicy and aromatic, it pairs beautifully with pumpkin and fruit.
- Cloves: Bold and intense, a little goes a long way.

2. Citrus Zest

Adding lemon or orange zest brightens fillings and balances richness.

3. Alcohol

Brandy, rum, or bourbon enhances flavors in pecan and mincemeat pies, adding depth and a festive twist.

Creative Holiday-Themed Decorations

1. Crust Designs
   - Lattice Top: Weave strips of dough for a classic look.
   - Shaped Cutouts: Use cookie cutters to make stars, snowflakes, or holly leaves from dough scraps.

2. Garnishes
   - Sugared Cranberries: Add a pop of color and sparkle.
   - Candied Pecans: Place a few on top of pecan pie for crunch and decoration.
   3. Seasonal Patterns
   - Use a knife to score freehand designs, like a Christmas tree or snowflakes, onto the top crust.

Tips for Perfect Holiday Pies

1. Prepare in Advance: Many holiday pies can be made a day or two ahead, giving you more time to enjoy the festivities.
   2. Serve Warm: Most pies taste best slightly warm—reheat them gently in the oven before serving.

3. Pair with Sides: Offer whipped cream, ice cream, or spiced custard for a complete dessert experience.

Conclusion

Holiday pies are more than just desserts—they're a celebration of flavor, tradition, and togetherness. Whether you're delighting in the spiced warmth of pumpkin pie, the buttery sweetness of pecan pie, or the rich complexity of mincemeat pie, these recipes and tips will help you create memorable pies that shine on your holiday table. Add a touch of creativity with festive decorations, and let your pies become the heart of your celebrations. Next, we'll explore savory pies that bring warmth and comfort to your kitchen. Let's keep baking!

Chapter 8: Classic Pot Pies

Savory pies, with their golden crusts and hearty fillings, bring comfort and warmth to any table. Among these, pot pies stand out as classics, celebrated for their rich, creamy fillings and satisfying textures. From traditional chicken pot pie to the robust flavors of beef and mushroom pie, and even vegetarian options brimming with seasonal vegetables, pot pies are a versatile dish perfect for weeknight meals or special occasions.

In this chapter, we'll explore detailed recipes for three classic pot pies, share techniques for achieving the perfect thick filling, and discuss the differences between puff pastry and traditional pastry crusts. Whether you're an experienced baker or a pot pie novice, this guide will help you craft the ultimate savory pie.

The Appeal of Pot Pies

1. A Meal in Itself

Pot pies combine protein, vegetables, and a rich sauce, all encased in a buttery crust, making them a complete meal.

2. Customizable and Versatile

Pot pies can be tailored to your preferences, accommodating various proteins, vegetables, and dietary restrictions.

3. Comfort Food at Its Best

With their warm, creamy fillings and flaky crusts, pot pies are the ultimate comfort food, evoking memories of home and family gatherings.

Recipes

1. Classic Chicken Pot Pie

A quintessential comfort food, chicken pot pie combines tender chicken with a medley of vegetables in a creamy sauce, all encased in a flaky crust.

Ingredients (Serves 6):

For the Filling:

- 2 tablespoons unsalted butter
- 2 tablespoons olive oil
- 1 small onion, diced
- 2 medium carrots, diced
- 2 celery stalks, diced
- 3 cloves garlic, minced
- 1/3 cup all-purpose flour
- 2 cups chicken broth
- 1 cup whole milk or heavy cream
- 3 cups cooked, shredded chicken
- 1 cup frozen peas
- 1 teaspoon dried thyme
- Salt and pepper, to taste
For the Crust:
- 1 unbaked pie crust or 1 sheet of puff pastry
- 1 egg, beaten (for egg wash)

Instructions:

1. Prepare the Filling:

- In a large skillet, heat butter and olive oil over medium heat. Sauté onion, carrots, and celery until softened (5–7 minutes). Add garlic and cook for 1 minute.

- Stir in flour and cook for 2 minutes to form a roux. Slowly whisk in chicken broth and milk, stirring constantly until the mixture thickens.

- Add shredded chicken, peas, thyme, salt, and pepper. Mix well and let cool slightly.

2. Assemble the Pie:

- Preheat oven to 375°F. Transfer the filling to a 9-inch pie dish. Cover with the crust, crimping the edges to seal. Cut slits in the top for ventilation. Brush with egg wash.

3. Bake:

- Bake for 30–35 minutes, or until the crust is golden brown. Let cool for 10 minutes before serving.

Pro Tip: For a richer flavor, substitute heavy cream for milk and add a splash of white wine to the filling.

2. Beef and Mushroom Pot Pie

This hearty pot pie features tender beef, earthy mushrooms, and a rich gravy, making it perfect for cooler months.

Ingredients (Serves 6):

For the Filling:

- 1 pound beef chuck, cubed
- 2 tablespoons all-purpose flour
- 2 tablespoons olive oil
- 1 small onion, diced
- 2 garlic cloves, minced
- 2 cups mushrooms, sliced
- 1 cup beef broth
- 1/2 cup red wine
- 2 tablespoons tomato paste
- 1 teaspoon dried rosemary
- 1 teaspoon dried thyme
- Salt and pepper, to taste

For the Crust:

- 1 unbaked pie crust or 1 sheet of puff pastry
- 1 egg, beaten (for egg wash)

Instructions:

1. Prepare the Filling:

- Toss beef cubes in flour, salt, and pepper. Heat olive oil in a skillet and sear the beef until browned. Remove and set aside.

- In the same skillet, sauté onion and garlic until softened. Add mushrooms and cook until tender. Stir in tomato paste and cook for 1 minute.

- Return beef to the skillet. Add beef broth, red wine, rosemary, and thyme. Simmer for 20–25 minutes, or until the liquid reduces and thickens.

2. Assemble the Pie:

- Preheat oven to 375°F. Transfer the filling to a 9-inch pie dish. Cover with the crust, crimping the edges to seal. Cut slits in the top for ventilation. Brush with egg wash.

3. Bake:

- Bake for 35–40 minutes, or until the crust is golden. Let cool slightly before serving.

Pro Tip: Add a splash of Worcestershire sauce to the filling for an extra depth of flavor.

3. Vegetarian Pot Pie

Packed with fresh vegetables and a creamy herb sauce, this vegetarian pot pie is a lighter yet satisfying option.

Ingredients (Serves 6):

For the Filling:

- 2 tablespoons unsalted butter
- 2 tablespoons olive oil
- 1 small onion, diced
- 2 medium carrots, diced
- 1 cup diced potatoes
- 1 cup broccoli florets
- 1/2 cup green beans, chopped
- 3 cloves garlic, minced
- 1/3 cup all-purpose flour
- 2 cups vegetable broth
- 1 cup whole milk or cream
- 1 teaspoon dried thyme
- Salt and pepper, to taste

For the Crust:

- 1 unbaked pie crust or 1 sheet of puff pastry
- 1 egg, beaten (for egg wash)

Instructions:

1. Prepare the Filling:

- Heat butter and olive oil in a skillet over medium heat. Sauté onion, carrots, and potatoes until softened (8–10 minutes). Add broccoli and green beans, cooking for 5 minutes.

- Stir in garlic and cook for 1 minute. Sprinkle with flour and cook for 2 minutes. Gradually whisk in vegetable broth and milk, stirring until thickened. Add thyme, salt, and pepper.

2. Assemble the Pie:

- Preheat oven to 375°F. Transfer the filling to a 9-inch pie dish. Cover with the crust, crimping the edges to seal. Cut slits in the top for ventilation. Brush with egg wash.

3. Bake:

- Bake for 30–35 minutes, or until the crust is golden brown. Let cool before serving.

Pro Tip: Customize the filling with seasonal vegetables like butternut squash in fall or zucchini in summer.

Tips for Thickening Savory Fillings

1. Use a Roux

A roux (a mixture of fat and flour) creates a creamy, thick base for your filling. Cook it thoroughly to avoid a raw flour taste.

2. Add Starch

- Cornstarch: Dissolve in cold broth or water before adding to the filling.

- Arrowroot Powder: A gluten-free thickener with a neutral flavor.

3. Simmer for Reduction

Allow your filling to simmer and reduce, which naturally thickens the sauce and intensifies flavors.

Crust Options: Puff Pastry vs. Traditional Pastry

Puff Pastry

- Pros: Buttery, flaky, and light, puff pastry creates an elegant topping for pot pies.
    - Cons: Can be more fragile and harder to handle than traditional pastry.
    Best Use: For individual pot pies or when a lighter crust is desired.

Traditional Pastry

- Pros: Sturdy, buttery, and easy to work with, it holds up well to heavier fillings.
    - Cons: May lack the delicate flakiness of puff pastry.
    Best Use: For classic pot pies with rich, hearty fillings.

Conclusion

Classic pot pies bring together the best of comfort food: tender fillings, savory sauces, and golden crusts. Whether you're enjoying a creamy chicken pot pie, a robust beef and mushroom pie, or a vibrant vegetarian version, the recipes and techniques in this chapter will help you create savory pies that are as satisfying as they are delicious. With the choice of puff pastry or traditional crust and tips for achieving the perfect thick filling, your pot pies are sure to become family favorites. Let's continue exploring savory pies with quiches and tarts in the next chapter!

Chapter 9: Quiches and Tarts

Quiches and savory tarts are versatile, elegant dishes that have earned their place in both casual brunches and formal dinners. A perfectly balanced quiche combines a creamy, flavorful custard with savory fillings, all nestled in a buttery crust. Tarts, with their crisp shells and refined presentations, offer endless possibilities for showcasing fresh, seasonal ingredients.

This chapter will guide you through creating three classic recipes: spinach and feta quiche, caramelized onion tart, and quiche Lorraine. You'll learn how to balance creamy custards with savory fillings, master the art of pre-baking crusts to avoid sogginess, and achieve flawless textures and flavors every time.

The Essentials of Quiches and Tarts

1. What Are Quiches and Tarts?

- Quiches: A custard-based savory pie with a rich filling, typically baked in a shortcrust pastry shell.

  - Tarts: Can be savory or sweet, with an emphasis on delicate crusts and artistic presentation.

2. The Importance of Custard

The custard is the heart of any quiche, providing a creamy, luscious base for the fillings. The key to a great custard is achieving the perfect balance of eggs and dairy.

Custard Ratio:

- For a classic quiche, use 1 egg for every 1/2 cup of dairy.
  - Use whole milk, heavy cream, or a combination of both for richness.

3. The Crust

A crisp, buttery crust is essential for quiches and tarts. Pre-baking, or blind baking, the crust ensures it stays firm and prevents sogginess once the filling is added.

Techniques for Perfect Quiches and Tarts

1. Pre-Baking the Crust

Pre-baking the crust ensures a firm, crisp base that won't absorb excess moisture from the filling.

Steps for Pre-Baking:

1. Prepare the Dough: Roll out your pastry dough and fit it into a tart or quiche pan. Trim the edges for a clean finish.

2. Chill: Refrigerate the crust for at least 30 minutes to prevent shrinking during baking.

3. Line and Weigh: Line the crust with parchment paper or foil and fill it with pie weights or dried beans to prevent bubbling.

4. Bake: Bake at 375°F (190°C) for 15 minutes. Remove the weights and parchment, then bake for another 5–7 minutes until lightly golden.

5. Cool: Allow the crust to cool slightly before adding the filling.

2. Balancing Fillings

- Use a combination of textures and flavors to create a harmonious dish.
- Avoid overloading the quiche or tart with too many ingredients, which can affect the custard's ability to set properly.

3. Even Baking

- Bake quiches and tarts on the middle rack for even heat distribution.

- The filling should be set but slightly jiggly in the center when removed from the oven.

Recipes

1. Spinach and Feta Quiche

This quiche combines the earthy flavors of spinach with the tangy creaminess of feta cheese, making it a crowd-pleaser for any meal.

Ingredients (Serves 6):

For the Crust:

- 1 unbaked shortcrust pastry (homemade or store-bought)

For the Filling:

- 1 tablespoon olive oil

- 1 small onion, finely diced

- 2 cups fresh spinach, chopped

- 3 large eggs

- 1 cup whole milk

- 1/2 cup heavy cream

- 1/2 cup crumbled feta cheese

- 1/4 teaspoon nutmeg

- Salt and pepper, to taste

Instructions:

1. Prepare the Crust:

- Roll out the shortcrust pastry and fit it into a 9-inch tart or quiche pan. Pre-bake the crust following the steps above.

2. Cook the Spinach:

- Heat olive oil in a skillet over medium heat. Sauté onion until translucent. Add spinach and cook until wilted. Season with salt and pepper. Let cool.

3. Make the Custard:

- In a bowl, whisk together eggs, milk, cream, nutmeg, salt, and pepper.

4. Assemble the Quiche:

- Spread the spinach mixture evenly in the pre-baked crust. Sprinkle feta cheese on top. Pour the custard over the fillings.

5. Bake:

- Preheat oven to 375°F (190°C). Bake for 35–40 minutes, or until the custard is set and the top is lightly golden. Cool slightly before serving.

Pro Tip: Add a pinch of red pepper flakes for a subtle kick.

2. Caramelized Onion Tart

Rich and flavorful, this tart highlights the natural sweetness of caramelized onions, balanced with a hint of thyme.

Ingredients (Serves 6):

For the Crust:

- 1 unbaked tart crust (homemade or store-bought)

For the Filling:

- 2 tablespoons unsalted butter

- 4 large onions, thinly sliced

- 1 teaspoon sugar

- 1 teaspoon fresh thyme leaves (or 1/2 teaspoon dried thyme)

- 3 large eggs

- 1/2 cup heavy cream

- 1/2 cup whole milk

- 1/2 cup grated Gruyère or Parmesan cheese

- Salt and pepper, to taste

Instructions:

1. Prepare the Crust:

- Roll out the tart crust and fit it into a 9-inch tart pan. Pre-bake the crust following the steps above.

2. Caramelize the Onions:

- Melt butter in a skillet over medium heat. Add onions and sugar, and cook, stirring occasionally, until deeply caramelized (about 25 minutes). Add thyme and season with salt and pepper. Let cool.

3. Make the Custard:

- In a bowl, whisk together eggs, cream, milk, salt, and pepper.

4. Assemble the Tart:

- Spread the caramelized onions in the pre-baked crust. Sprinkle with cheese. Pour the custard over the onions.

5. Bake:

- Preheat oven to 375°F (190°C). Bake for 30–35 minutes, or until the custard is set and the top is golden. Cool slightly before serving.

Pro Tip: Garnish with fresh thyme sprigs for an elegant presentation.

3. Quiche Lorraine

A French classic, quiche Lorraine features smoky bacon and Gruyère cheese in a creamy custard.

Ingredients (Serves 6):

For the Crust:

- 1 unbaked shortcrust pastry (homemade or store-bought)

For the Filling:

- 6 slices bacon, cooked and crumbled

- 1 small onion, finely diced

- 3 large eggs

- 1 cup whole milk

- 1/2 cup heavy cream

- 1/2 cup grated Gruyère cheese

- Salt and pepper, to taste

Instructions:

1. Prepare the Crust:

- Roll out the shortcrust pastry and fit it into a 9-inch tart or quiche pan. Pre-bake the crust following the steps above.

2. Cook the Bacon and Onion:

- Sauté onion in a skillet until softened. Mix with cooked, crumbled bacon.

3. Make the Custard:

- In a bowl, whisk together eggs, milk, cream, salt, and pepper.

4. Assemble the Quiche:

- Spread the bacon and onion mixture evenly in the pre-baked crust. Sprinkle with Gruyère cheese. Pour the custard over the fillings.

5. Bake:

- Preheat oven to 375°F (190°C). Bake for 35–40 minutes, or until the custard is set and the top is lightly browned. Cool slightly before serving.

Pro Tip: Substitute pancetta for bacon for a more authentic flavor.

Tips for Perfect Quiches and Tarts

1. Preventing Soggy Crusts

- Always pre-bake your crust.

- Brush the crust with an egg wash before adding the filling to create a barrier.

2. Avoiding Overcooking

- Remove the quiche or tart from the oven when the center is still slightly jiggly; it will continue to set as it cools.

3. Enhancing Presentation

- Use decorative fluted tart pans for an elegant look.

- Garnish with fresh herbs or edible flowers before serving.

Conclusion

Quiches and tarts are timeless dishes that combine rich, creamy custards with flavorful fillings and crisp crusts. Whether you're making a classic quiche Lorraine, a sophisticated caramelized onion tart, or a vibrant spinach and feta quiche, these recipes and techniques will help you achieve perfection. With attention to detail and a touch of creativity, your quiches and tarts will become the centerpiece of any table. Let's continue exploring savory pies with the next chapter on meat-filled delights!

Chapter 10: Meat Pies from Around the World

Meat pies are a beloved culinary tradition across the globe, each region showcasing its unique flavors, techniques, and ingredients. These savory pies offer a satisfying combination of rich, flavorful fillings encased in golden, flaky crusts. Whether it's the hearty tourtière from Canada, the robust steak and kidney pie from the UK, or the portable and versatile empanadas of Latin America, meat pies are a celebration of culture and comfort.

In this chapter, we'll explore three iconic meat pie recipes, delve into the regional variations and flavor profiles that make each one unique, and share expert tips for sealing and baking your meat pies to perfection.

The Universal Appeal of Meat Pies

Meat pies have been cherished for centuries, providing a portable and nourishing meal for farmers, workers, and travelers. They are as diverse as the cultures that create them, with each variation reflecting local ingredients and culinary traditions.

1. Historical Significance

- Meat pies date back to ancient civilizations, where crusts served as edible containers to preserve fillings.

- Over time, these pies evolved into staples of home cooking, street food, and even high-end cuisine.

2. Versatility

- Meat pies can be adapted to use whatever meats, vegetables, and spices are on hand, making them a practical and resourceful dish.

3. Cultural Identity

- Each meat pie carries the essence of its culture, from the spices used to the methods of preparation and presentation.

Techniques for Perfect Meat Pies

1. The Importance of a Good Crust
   - The crust should be sturdy enough to hold the filling but tender and flaky for a delightful texture.
   - Use cold butter or lard and handle the dough minimally to achieve the desired flakiness.
   2. Thickening the Filling
   - A thick filling ensures the pie holds its shape when sliced or bitten into.
   - Common thickeners include flour, cornstarch, or a reduction of the filling's liquid.
   3. Sealing the Edges
   - Proper sealing prevents the filling from leaking during baking.
   - Techniques include crimping with a fork, pinching with fingers, or using decorative edge cutters.
   4. Venting the Pie
   - Cutting slits or adding decorative vents allows steam to escape, preventing soggy crusts.

Recipes

1. Tourtière (Canada)

A traditional French-Canadian meat pie, tourtière is a holiday favorite made with a flavorful blend of ground meats and warm spices.

Ingredients (Serves 6):

For the Crust:

- 2 1/2 cups all-purpose flour
- 1 teaspoon salt
- 1 cup cold unsalted butter, cubed
- 6-8 tablespoons ice water

For the Filling:

- 1 tablespoon olive oil
- 1 medium onion, finely diced
- 2 cloves garlic, minced
- 1 pound ground pork (or a mix of pork and beef)
- 1/2 teaspoon ground cinnamon
- 1/4 teaspoon ground cloves
- 1/4 teaspoon ground allspice
- 1/4 cup chicken or beef broth
- Salt and pepper, to taste
- 1 medium potato, boiled and mashed
For Assembly:
- 1 egg, beaten (for egg wash)
Instructions:
1. Prepare the Crust:
- Combine flour and salt in a bowl. Cut in cold butter until the mixture resembles coarse crumbs. Add ice water, one tablespoon at a time, mixing until the dough just comes together. Divide into two discs, wrap in plastic, and chill for 30 minutes.
2. Make the Filling:
- Heat olive oil in a skillet over medium heat. Sauté onion and garlic until softened. Add ground meat, breaking it up with a spoon, and cook until browned. Stir in cinnamon, cloves, allspice, salt, and pepper. Add broth and simmer until most of the liquid is absorbed. Mix in mashed potato and let cool.
3. Assemble the Pie:
- Roll out one dough disc and line a 9-inch pie dish. Fill with the meat mixture. Roll out the second disc and place it over the filling. Trim and crimp the edges. Cut slits for ventilation and brush with egg wash.
4. Bake:
- Preheat oven to 375°F (190°C). Bake for 35–40 minutes, or until the crust is golden brown. Let cool slightly before serving.
Pro Tip: Serve tourtière with a side of tangy ketchup or fruit chutney to enhance the flavors.

2. Steak and Kidney Pie (UK)

A classic British comfort food, steak and kidney pie features tender beef, kidneys, and a rich gravy encased in a buttery crust.

Ingredients (Serves 6):

For the Crust:

- 1 1/2 cups all-purpose flour

- 1/2 teaspoon salt

- 1/2 cup cold butter, cubed

- 3-4 tablespoons ice water

For the Filling:

- 1 tablespoon vegetable oil

- 1 pound stewing beef, cubed

- 1/2 pound lamb or beef kidney, trimmed and chopped

- 1 medium onion, diced

- 1 cup mushrooms, sliced

- 2 tablespoons all-purpose flour

- 1 1/2 cups beef broth

- 1/4 cup red wine

- 1 teaspoon Worcestershire sauce

- 1 teaspoon dried thyme

- Salt and pepper, to taste

For Assembly:

- 1 egg, beaten (for egg wash)

Instructions:

1. Prepare the Crust:

- Combine flour and salt in a bowl. Cut in cold butter until crumbly. Add ice water until the dough forms a ball. Chill for 30 minutes.

2. Make the Filling:

- Heat oil in a skillet. Brown beef and kidneys, then remove and set aside. Sauté onion and mushrooms until softened. Sprinkle with flour and cook for 2 minutes. Return meat to the skillet, add broth, wine, Worcestershire sauce, thyme, salt, and pepper. Simmer until thickened.

3. Assemble the Pie:

- Roll out the dough and line a pie dish. Pour in the filling. Roll out remaining dough and cover the pie. Trim, crimp edges, and cut slits for steam. Brush with egg wash.

4. Bake:

- Preheat oven to 400°F (200°C). Bake for 30–35 minutes, or until golden brown. Cool slightly before serving.

Pro Tip: Substitute kidneys with mushrooms for a kidney-free version with similar depth of flavor.

3. Empanadas (Latin America)

Empanadas are hand-held meat pies with a variety of fillings, from seasoned beef to chicken or even seafood.

Ingredients (Makes 12 Empanadas):

For the Dough:

- 2 1/2 cups all-purpose flour
- 1 teaspoon salt
- 1/2 cup unsalted butter, chilled and cubed
- 1 egg
- 1/4 cup ice water

For the Filling:

- 1 tablespoon olive oil
- 1 small onion, diced
- 1/2 pound ground beef
- 1/4 cup diced olives
- 1/4 cup raisins
- 1 teaspoon paprika
- 1/2 teaspoon cumin
- Salt and pepper, to taste

For Assembly:

- 1 egg, beaten (for egg wash)

Instructions:

1. Prepare the Dough:

- Combine flour and salt. Cut in butter until the mixture resembles crumbs. Add egg and ice water, mixing until a dough forms. Chill for 30 minutes.

2. Make the Filling:

- Heat olive oil in a skillet. Cook onion until softened, then add ground beef. Stir in olives, raisins, paprika, cumin, salt, and pepper. Let cool.

3. Assemble the Empanadas:

- Roll out dough and cut into 5-inch circles. Place a spoonful of filling in the center. Fold in half and crimp edges to seal. Brush with egg wash.

4. Bake:

- Preheat oven to 375°F (190°C). Bake for 20–25 minutes, or until golden brown.

Pro Tip: For a crispier texture, fry the empanadas instead of baking them.

Regional Variations and Flavor Profiles

1. Tourtière Variations
   - Seafood Tourtière: Common in coastal areas, featuring scallops or fish.
   - Vegetarian Tourtière: Substitutes meat with lentils, mushrooms, or chickpeas.
2. Steak and Kidney Pie Variations
   - Steak and Ale Pie: Uses ale instead of wine for a deeper flavor.
   - Chicken and Leek Pie: A lighter alternative with a creamy sauce.
3. Empanada Variations
   - Argentinian Empanadas: Include hard-boiled eggs and paprika-rich fillings.
   - Colombian Empanadas: Use cornmeal dough and often feature spiced potatoes.

Tips for Sealing and Baking Meat Pies

1. Chill the Dough: Cold dough is easier to handle and holds its shape better during baking.

2. Use an Egg Wash: This creates a golden, glossy finish and helps seal the edges.

3. Allow Resting Time: Let pies cool slightly before slicing to prevent the filling from spilling out.

Conclusion

Meat pies are a celebration of global culinary traditions, showcasing the flavors and techniques of diverse cultures. From the spiced warmth of a Canadian tourtière to the hearty richness of a British steak and kidney pie and the portable delight of Latin American empanadas, these pies offer something for every taste and occasion. With the recipes, tips, and techniques shared in this chapter, you'll master the art of crafting meat pies that are as delicious as they are authentic. Let's continue our pie journey with sweet indulgences in the next chapter!

Chapter 11: No-Bake Pies

No-bake pies are a testament to simplicity and creativity in dessert-making. These pies skip the oven entirely, relying on refrigeration or freezing to set the filling, making them ideal for warm-weather treats or quick dessert solutions. From the tangy elegance of key lime pie to the indulgent richness of peanut butter pie and the refreshing delight of frozen berry pie, no-bake pies offer versatility, flavor, and ease.

This chapter explores three standout recipes, delves into techniques for achieving firm fillings without baking, and introduces creative ideas for cookie and nut-based crusts. Whether you're looking to impress guests or satisfy a sweet craving without turning on the oven, no-bake pies are the perfect solution.

Why Choose No-Bake Pies?

1. Convenience

No-bake pies require minimal preparation and no oven time, making them ideal for hot days or when you're short on time.

2. Versatility

These pies can be adapted to suit a variety of flavors, dietary preferences, and occasions. They're also highly customizable with different crusts and fillings.

3. Refreshing and Light

Often chilled or frozen, no-bake pies are refreshing, making them a popular choice for spring and summer desserts.

Techniques for Firm Fillings

Achieving the perfect set for a no-bake pie depends on the right ingredients and techniques. Here's how to ensure your fillings are firm yet creamy:

1. Use Stabilizers
   - Gelatin: Provides structure and stability to creamy fillings.
   - Whipped Cream: Adds lightness while helping the filling hold its shape.
   - Cream Cheese: Common in no-bake pies, cream cheese lends a thick, creamy texture.
   2. Refrigeration and Freezing
   - Chill the pie for at least 4–6 hours, or overnight, to allow the filling to set fully.
   - For frozen pies, ensure they are kept in the freezer for the specified time and thaw slightly before serving.
   3. Proper Ratios
   - Use the right balance of liquid and thickening agents to avoid a runny filling. For example, in cream-based pies, equal parts cream cheese and whipped cream often yield the best consistency.

Creative Crusts

No-bake pies often feature cookie or nut-based crusts, which are quick to prepare and full of flavor. These crusts require only a bit of chilling to set, eliminating the need for baking.
   1. Cookie Crusts
   - Graham Cracker Crust: A classic choice for many no-bake pies, made by combining crushed graham crackers, sugar, and melted butter.
   - Oreo Crust: Perfect for chocolate-based pies, made from crushed Oreo cookies and melted butter.
   2. Nut-Based Crusts
   - Almond Crust: Ground almonds mixed with a bit of sugar and butter create a nutty, crunchy base.
   - Pecan Crust: Toasted pecans add depth and flavor to creamy fillings.
   3. Combination Crusts
   - Mix crushed cookies with ground nuts for a unique, textured crust.
   Recipes

1. Key Lime Pie

A tangy, creamy classic, key lime pie is the epitome of refreshing desserts. This no-bake version is easy to prepare and perfect for any occasion.

Ingredients (Serves 8):

For the Crust:

- 1 1/2 cups graham cracker crumbs

- 1/4 cup granulated sugar

- 6 tablespoons unsalted butter, melted

For the Filling:

- 1 can (14 ounces) sweetened condensed milk

- 1/2 cup freshly squeezed key lime juice

- 1 teaspoon lime zest

- 1 cup heavy cream, whipped to stiff peaks

For Garnish:

- Whipped cream

- Lime slices or zest

Instructions:

1. Prepare the Crust:

- Mix graham cracker crumbs, sugar, and melted butter in a bowl. Press the mixture evenly into the bottom and up the sides of a 9-inch pie dish. Chill for 15 minutes.

2. Make the Filling:

- In a bowl, whisk together sweetened condensed milk, lime juice, and lime zest. Gently fold in whipped cream until smooth.

3. Assemble the Pie:

- Pour the filling into the chilled crust. Smooth the top and refrigerate for at least 4 hours, or until firm.

4. Garnish and Serve:

- Top with whipped cream and lime slices or zest before serving.

Pro Tip: For a burst of flavor, substitute part of the lime juice with lemon juice for a citrusy twist.

2. Peanut Butter Pie

Rich and indulgent, peanut butter pie is a decadent no-bake dessert that's sure to satisfy any sweet tooth.

Ingredients (Serves 8):

For the Crust:

- 1 1/2 cups crushed Oreo cookies

- 5 tablespoons unsalted butter, melted

For the Filling:

- 1 cup creamy peanut butter

- 1 package (8 ounces) cream cheese, softened

- 1 cup powdered sugar

- 1 cup heavy cream, whipped to stiff peaks

For Garnish:

- Chopped peanuts

- Chocolate shavings

Instructions:

1. Prepare the Crust:

- Combine crushed Oreos and melted butter in a bowl. Press the mixture into a 9-inch pie dish. Chill for 15 minutes.

2. Make the Filling:

- Beat peanut butter, cream cheese, and powdered sugar in a bowl until smooth. Gently fold in whipped cream.

3. Assemble the Pie:

- Spread the filling evenly into the chilled crust. Refrigerate for at least 4 hours, or until set.

4. Garnish and Serve:

- Top with chopped peanuts and chocolate shavings before serving.

Pro Tip: Drizzle melted chocolate over the filling for an added touch of decadence.

3. Frozen Berry Pie

This pie is a summer favorite, featuring a medley of frozen berries in a creamy base. It's a vibrant and refreshing dessert perfect for hot days.

Ingredients (Serves 8):

For the Crust:

- 1 1/2 cups crushed digestive biscuits

- 6 tablespoons unsalted butter, melted

For the Filling:

- 2 cups mixed frozen berries (blueberries, raspberries, strawberries)

- 1/2 cup granulated sugar

- 1 teaspoon lemon juice

- 1 cup heavy cream, whipped to stiff peaks

- 1/2 cup Greek yogurt

For Garnish:

- Fresh berries

- Mint leaves

Instructions:

1. Prepare the Crust:

- Combine crushed biscuits and melted butter in a bowl. Press into a 9-inch pie dish. Chill for 15 minutes.

2. Make the Filling:

- In a saucepan, combine frozen berries, sugar, and lemon juice. Cook over medium heat until the berries release their juices and the mixture thickens. Let cool completely.

- Fold the berry mixture into whipped cream and Greek yogurt until combined.

3. Assemble the Pie:

- Spread the filling into the chilled crust. Freeze for at least 6 hours, or overnight.

4. Garnish and Serve:

- Decorate with fresh berries and mint leaves before serving.

Pro Tip: For a smoother texture, blend the berry mixture before folding it into the cream.

Tips for No-Bake Pie Success

1. Choose the Right Dish: Use a pie dish with removable sides for easy slicing and serving.

2. Chill Thoroughly: Give your pie enough time to set in the refrigerator or freezer for the best texture.

3. Decorate Thoughtfully: Whipped cream, fresh fruit, or chocolate shavings add a finishing touch that enhances both flavor and presentation.

Conclusion

No-bake pies are a delightful combination of simplicity, creativity, and flavor. Whether you're savoring the zesty tang of key lime pie, the creamy decadence of peanut butter pie, or the refreshing burst of a frozen berry pie, these recipes are guaranteed to impress. With firm fillings, versatile crusts, and minimal effort, no-bake pies are the perfect addition to any dessert repertoire. Let's continue our journey into modern pies with a focus on deconstructed and plated creations in the next chapter!

Chapter 12: Hand Pies and Mini Pies

Hand pies and mini pies are delightful, portable versions of traditional pies, offering convenience without sacrificing flavor. These small-scale creations are perfect for casual snacking, parties, and gift-giving, showcasing the same rich fillings and flaky crusts of their full-sized counterparts in a more personal and portable format.

In this chapter, we'll explore detailed recipes for blueberry hand pies, savory hand pies, and mini pecan pies. You'll learn techniques to perfect portability while maintaining robust flavors and discover decorative methods to elevate these small-scale pies into works of art.

The Appeal of Hand Pies and Mini Pies

1. Versatility and Portability
   - Hand pies and mini pies are easy to transport, making them perfect for picnics, potlucks, and lunchboxes.
   - They can be sweet or savory, catering to a variety of tastes and occasions.
2. Portion Control
   - These smaller pies allow for perfectly portioned servings, ideal for individual enjoyment.
3. Aesthetic Appeal
   - With creative designs and decorative techniques, hand pies and mini pies are visually stunning, perfect for gifting or entertaining.

Techniques for Perfect Hand Pies and Mini Pies

1. Choosing the Right Dough
   - All-Butter Pie Crust: Provides a flaky texture and rich flavor.
   - Puff Pastry: Creates a light, airy crust that works well for sweet or savory hand pies.

- Shortcrust Pastry: Offers sturdiness for holding fillings without leaking.

2. Sealing the Edges

- Use a fork to crimp the edges of hand pies for a rustic look and a secure seal.

- For mini pies, press the edges firmly into the tin to ensure the filling stays enclosed.

3. Preventing Leakage

- Avoid overfilling to prevent the pies from bursting during baking.

- Use a small egg wash on the edges before sealing to create a strong bond.

4. Venting and Glazing

- Add small slits or decorative cuts to hand pies to allow steam to escape.

- Brush with an egg wash for a golden, glossy finish or sprinkle with sugar for added texture.

Recipes

1. Blueberry Hand Pies

Bursting with sweet, juicy blueberries and encased in a flaky crust, blueberry hand pies are a timeless treat.

Ingredients (Makes 10 Hand Pies):

For the Dough:

- 2 1/2 cups all-purpose flour

- 1 teaspoon salt

- 1 tablespoon granulated sugar

- 1 cup unsalted butter, chilled and cubed

- 6-8 tablespoons ice water

For the Filling:

- 2 cups fresh or frozen blueberries

- 1/4 cup granulated sugar

- 1 tablespoon cornstarch

- 1 teaspoon lemon juice

- 1/2 teaspoon vanilla extract

For Assembly:

- 1 egg, beaten (for egg wash)

- Turbinado sugar (optional, for sprinkling)

Instructions:

1. Prepare the Dough:

- In a large bowl, mix flour, salt, and sugar. Cut in butter until the mixture resembles coarse crumbs. Add ice water, one tablespoon at a time, until the dough comes together. Divide into two discs, wrap in plastic, and chill for 30 minutes.

2. Make the Filling:

- Combine blueberries, sugar, cornstarch, lemon juice, and vanilla extract in a saucepan. Cook over medium heat until thickened, about 5 minutes. Let cool.

3. Assemble the Hand Pies:

- Preheat oven to 375°F (190°C). Roll out the dough to 1/8-inch thickness. Cut out 4-inch circles. Place a spoonful of filling in the center of each circle. Fold in half and crimp the edges with a fork.

4. Bake:

- Brush the pies with egg wash and sprinkle with turbinado sugar. Bake for 20–25 minutes, or until golden brown. Cool on a wire rack before serving.

Pro Tip: Serve with a dollop of whipped cream or vanilla ice cream for extra indulgence.

2. Savory Hand Pies

Savory hand pies are a satisfying meal on the go, filled with hearty ingredients like meat, vegetables, or cheese.

Ingredients (Makes 10 Hand Pies):

For the Dough:

- 2 1/2 cups all-purpose flour

- 1 teaspoon salt

- 1 cup cold unsalted butter, cubed
- 6-8 tablespoons ice water
For the Filling:
- 1 tablespoon olive oil
- 1 small onion, diced
- 1/2 pound ground beef or turkey
- 1/2 cup diced carrots
- 1/2 cup peas
- 1 teaspoon Worcestershire sauce
- Salt and pepper, to taste
For Assembly:
- 1 egg, beaten (for egg wash)
Instructions:
1. Prepare the Dough:
- Follow the same method as for the blueberry hand pies.
2. Make the Filling:
- Heat olive oil in a skillet over medium heat. Cook onion until softened. Add ground meat, carrots, and peas. Season with Worcestershire sauce, salt, and pepper. Cook until the meat is browned and the vegetables are tender. Let cool.
3. Assemble the Hand Pies:
- Roll out the dough and cut into circles or squares. Place a spoonful of filling in the center, fold, and seal the edges with a fork.
4. Bake:
- Preheat oven to 375°F (190°C). Brush with egg wash and bake for 25–30 minutes, or until golden brown.
Pro Tip: Add shredded cheese to the filling for an extra layer of flavor.

3. Mini Pecan Pies

These bite-sized treats capture the rich, nutty sweetness of pecan pie in a portable format.
Ingredients (Makes 12 Mini Pies):
For the Crust:
- 1 1/4 cups all-purpose flour

- 1/2 teaspoon salt
- 1/2 cup cold unsalted butter, cubed
- 3-4 tablespoons ice water
For the Filling:
- 3/4 cup brown sugar
- 1/2 cup light corn syrup
- 2 large eggs
- 2 tablespoons unsalted butter, melted
- 1 teaspoon vanilla extract
- 1 cup chopped pecans
Instructions:
1. Prepare the Crust:
- Combine flour and salt in a bowl. Cut in butter until crumbly. Add ice water until the dough forms a ball. Chill for 30 minutes.
2. Make the Filling:
- In a bowl, whisk together brown sugar, corn syrup, eggs, melted butter, and vanilla extract. Stir in chopped pecans.
3. Assemble the Mini Pies:
- Preheat oven to 350°F (175°C). Roll out the dough and cut into small circles. Fit each circle into the cups of a mini muffin tin. Spoon the filling into each crust.
4. Bake:
- Bake for 20–25 minutes, or until the filling is set and the crust is golden. Cool before removing from the tin.
Pro Tip: Top each mini pie with a whole pecan for a decorative finish.

Decorative Techniques for Small-Scale Pies

1. Crimped Edges
- Use a fork to create a simple, rustic edge or pinch the dough with your fingers for a scalloped design.
2. Lattice Tops

- For mini pies, use thin strips of dough to create a lattice pattern over the filling.

3. Stamped Shapes

- Use small cookie cutters to create decorative shapes from extra dough and place them on top of the pies.

4. Egg Wash and Sugar

- Brush with an egg wash for a golden finish and sprinkle with coarse sugar for added texture.

Conclusion

Hand pies and mini pies combine the comfort of traditional pies with the convenience of individual servings. Whether you're savoring a sweet blueberry hand pie, indulging in a rich mini pecan pie, or enjoying the hearty flavors of a savory hand pie, these recipes offer something for every occasion. With techniques for sealing, decorating, and perfecting the crust, you'll be able to create beautiful, flavorful small-scale pies that are as portable as they are delicious. Let's continue our exploration of creative pies with the next chapter on deconstructed and plated pies!

Chapter 13: Vegan and Gluten-Free Pies

In recent years, vegan and gluten-free baking has gone from niche to mainstream, driven by dietary needs and a growing interest in plant-based and allergen-friendly cooking. Creating vegan and gluten-free pies may seem challenging, but with the right ingredients and techniques, these pies can be every bit as indulgent, flavorful, and satisfying as their traditional counterparts.

This chapter will explore three delicious recipes: vegan chocolate pie, gluten-free fruit pie, and coconut cream pie. You'll learn about substitutes for dairy, eggs, and gluten, as well as expert tips for maintaining texture and flavor in alternative pies. By the end, you'll have the confidence to craft pies that cater to various dietary preferences without compromising on taste or quality.

Why Vegan and Gluten-Free Pies Matter

1. Inclusivity
   - Vegan and gluten-free pies ensure everyone at the table can enjoy a delicious dessert, regardless of dietary restrictions.
   2. Health and Sustainability
   - Plant-based and gluten-free baking often incorporates whole, minimally processed ingredients, aligning with health-conscious and eco-friendly lifestyles.
   3. Creativity in Baking
   - Working with alternative ingredients challenges bakers to innovate, resulting in unique and delightful flavors.

Substitutes for Dairy, Eggs, and Gluten

1. Dairy Substitutes

- Milk: Almond milk, oat milk, soy milk, or coconut milk are excellent alternatives to dairy milk.

- Butter: Replace butter with coconut oil, vegan margarine, or plant-based butter.

- Cream: Coconut cream or cashew cream works well for rich fillings and toppings.

2. Egg Substitutes

- Flaxseed Meal or Chia Seeds: Mix 1 tablespoon of flaxseed or chia seed meal with 2 1/2 tablespoons of water to replace one egg.

- Silken Tofu: Use 1/4 cup of blended silken tofu for a creamy texture in custard-based pies.

- Aquafaba: The liquid from canned chickpeas can mimic egg whites in meringues or whipped fillings.

3. Gluten Substitutes

- Flour Blends: Use gluten-free all-purpose flour blends that contain a mix of rice flour, tapioca starch, and xanthan gum for structure.

- Nut and Oat Flours: Almond flour or oat flour can provide texture and flavor to gluten-free crusts.

- Binders: Xanthan gum or psyllium husk helps mimic the elasticity of gluten in doughs.

Tips for Maintaining Texture and Flavor

1. Don't Skip Resting Time: Gluten-free and vegan doughs often need time to hydrate and firm up before rolling. Chill them for at least 30 minutes.

2. Use a Gentle Hand: Overworking gluten-free dough can lead to crumbling. Handle it minimally to maintain structure.

3. Enhance Flavor with Additives: Add a pinch of salt, vanilla extract, or spices to enrich the flavor of alternative pie crusts and fillings.

4. Balance Moisture: Ensure your fillings have the right consistency to avoid soggy crusts or overly dry pies.

Recipes

1. Vegan Chocolate Pie

This luscious vegan chocolate pie uses rich, creamy ingredients to create a decadent dessert that's entirely plant-based.

Ingredients (Serves 8):

For the Crust:

- 1 1/2 cups crushed graham crackers (vegan)

- 1/4 cup coconut oil, melted

- 2 tablespoons maple syrup

For the Filling:

- 1 1/2 cups dairy-free dark chocolate chips

- 1 can (14 ounces) coconut cream

- 1/4 cup maple syrup

- 1 teaspoon vanilla extract

For Garnish:

- Shaved dark chocolate or fresh berries

Instructions:

1. Prepare the Crust:

- Mix crushed graham crackers, coconut oil, and maple syrup in a bowl. Press into a 9-inch pie dish. Chill for 15 minutes.

2. Make the Filling:

- Heat coconut cream in a saucepan until just simmering. Remove from heat and stir in chocolate chips until melted. Add maple syrup and vanilla extract, mixing until smooth.

3. Assemble the Pie:

- Pour the filling into the chilled crust. Smooth the top and refrigerate for at least 4 hours, or until set.

4. Garnish and Serve:

- Top with shaved chocolate or fresh berries before serving.

Pro Tip: For added flavor, mix a pinch of sea salt into the filling.

2. Gluten-Free Fruit Pie

This gluten-free fruit pie celebrates the vibrant flavors of seasonal fruits with a tender, flaky crust.

Ingredients (Serves 8):

For the Crust:

- 2 cups gluten-free all-purpose flour

- 1 teaspoon xanthan gum (if not included in the flour blend)

- 1/2 teaspoon salt

- 1/2 cup cold vegan butter or coconut oil

- 6-8 tablespoons ice water

For the Filling:

- 4 cups mixed berries (blueberries, raspberries, blackberries)

- 1/2 cup granulated sugar

- 2 tablespoons cornstarch

- 1 teaspoon lemon juice

For Assembly:

- 1 tablespoon almond milk (for brushing)

- Turbinado sugar (optional, for sprinkling)

Instructions:

1. Prepare the Crust:

- Mix gluten-free flour, xanthan gum, and salt in a bowl. Cut in butter until the mixture resembles coarse crumbs. Add ice water, one tablespoon at a time, until the dough comes together. Chill for 30 minutes.

2. Make the Filling:

- In a bowl, combine berries, sugar, cornstarch, and lemon juice. Toss to coat evenly.

3. Assemble the Pie:

- Preheat oven to 375°F (190°C). Roll out the dough and fit it into a 9-inch pie dish. Add the berry filling. Roll out remaining dough for the top crust, cutting slits for ventilation. Seal and crimp the edges. Brush with almond milk and sprinkle with turbinado sugar.

4. Bake:

- Bake for 40–45 minutes, or until the crust is golden brown and the filling is bubbling. Cool before serving.

Pro Tip: Use frozen fruit if fresh berries are unavailable; just increase the cornstarch slightly.

3. Coconut Cream Pie

This creamy, tropical pie is both vegan and gluten-free, offering a light and luscious dessert.

Ingredients (Serves 8):

For the Crust:

- 1 1/2 cups almond flour

- 1/4 cup coconut oil, melted

- 2 tablespoons maple syrup

For the Filling:

- 1 can (14 ounces) coconut milk

- 1/2 cup coconut cream

- 1/4 cup cornstarch

- 1/4 cup maple syrup

- 1 teaspoon vanilla extract

For Topping:

- Toasted coconut flakes

Instructions:

1. Prepare the Crust:

- Mix almond flour, coconut oil, and maple syrup in a bowl. Press into a 9-inch pie dish. Chill for 15 minutes.

2. Make the Filling:

- In a saucepan, whisk together coconut milk, coconut cream, cornstarch, and maple syrup. Cook over medium heat, stirring constantly, until thickened. Remove from heat and stir in vanilla extract.

3. Assemble the Pie:

- Pour the filling into the crust. Smooth the top and refrigerate for at least 4 hours, or until set.

4. Garnish and Serve:

- Top with toasted coconut flakes before serving.

Pro Tip: For an extra tropical twist, add a layer of sliced bananas before pouring in the filling.

Conclusion

Vegan and gluten-free pies showcase the creativity and adaptability of modern baking. Whether it's the decadent richness of vegan chocolate pie, the vibrant freshness of gluten-free fruit pie, or the tropical indulgence of coconut cream pie, these recipes prove that dietary restrictions don't mean compromising on flavor or quality. By mastering alternative ingredients and techniques, you'll be able to craft pies that delight every palate and celebrate inclusivity in baking. Let's move forward to explore deconstructed pies and plated presentations in the next chapter!

Chapter 14: Show-Stopping Party Pies

Pies are more than just desserts—they can be the centerpiece of a party, a conversation starter, and a visual masterpiece. Show-stopping pies elevate the humble dessert into edible art, using creative layering, intricate designs, and vibrant colors. Whether you're crafting a rainbow pie to celebrate a special occasion, a checkerboard pie to amaze your guests, or a decorative lattice fruit pie for seasonal charm, these visually stunning creations are guaranteed to leave an impression.

In this chapter, you'll learn recipes and techniques for crafting these extraordinary pies, along with tips for themed and seasonal presentations. From choosing the right colors to mastering intricate latticework, this guide will equip you with the skills to turn your pies into unforgettable showpieces.

Why Show-Stopping Pies?

1. Celebratory Atmosphere
   - A visually stunning pie enhances the festive feel of any gathering, from birthdays to weddings to holiday feasts.
   2. Personal Touch
   - Custom designs and themes allow you to tailor pies to specific events, making them unique and memorable.
   3. Creativity and Fun
   - Designing a show-stopping pie is an opportunity to unleash your creativity and have fun in the kitchen.

Key Techniques for Stunning Pies

1. Choosing the Right Ingredients
   - Use high-quality, fresh ingredients for the best flavor and visual appeal.
   - Vibrant fruits, natural food coloring, and smooth fillings create a polished look.
   2. Layering for Visual Impact
   - Colorful layers add depth and intrigue to pies like the rainbow pie.
   - Use transparent or light-colored fillings to let the layers shine.

3. Mastering Decorative Crusts

- Latticework, cutouts, and braided edges add texture and elegance to pies.

- Use pie dough cutters, stencils, and sharp knives for clean designs.

4. Balancing Aesthetics with Flavor

- Ensure that the pie's visual appeal doesn't compromise its taste. A show-stopping pie should be as delicious as it is beautiful.

Recipes

1. Layered Rainbow Pie

This vibrant, colorful pie is perfect for birthdays, Pride celebrations, or any festive occasion. Layers of smooth, colorful filling create a dazzling effect.

Ingredients (Serves 8):

For the Crust:

- 1 1/2 cups graham cracker crumbs

- 1/4 cup granulated sugar

- 6 tablespoons unsalted butter, melted

For the Filling:

- 4 cups whipped cream or whipped coconut cream

- 1/2 cup sweetened condensed milk (or coconut condensed milk for vegan)

- 6 different natural food colorings or fruit purées (e.g., strawberry, mango, blueberry, spinach)

- 1 teaspoon vanilla extract

Instructions:

1. Prepare the Crust:

- Combine graham cracker crumbs, sugar, and melted butter. Press into a 9-inch pie dish. Chill for 15 minutes.

2. Divide the Filling:

- In a large bowl, fold whipped cream into the sweetened condensed milk and vanilla extract. Divide into six equal portions. Mix each portion with a different food coloring or fruit purée.

3. Layer the Colors:

- Pour the first color into the pie crust, smoothing it evenly. Freeze for 15 minutes to set. Repeat with each color, freezing between layers.

4. Chill and Serve:

- Chill the finished pie for at least 4 hours, or overnight. Serve with whipped cream and rainbow sprinkles.

Pro Tip: Use a piping bag for even layers and sharp edges between colors.

2. Checkerboard Pie

A checkerboard pie combines two contrasting fillings in a striking pattern. This pie works well with sweet or savory combinations, such as cherry and chocolate or spinach and ricotta.

Ingredients (Serves 8):

For the Crust:

- 2 1/2 cups all-purpose flour

- 1 teaspoon salt

- 1 cup unsalted butter, cubed and chilled

- 6-8 tablespoons ice water

For the Filling (Sweet Option):

- 2 cups cherry pie filling

- 2 cups chocolate custard

For the Filling (Savory Option):

- 2 cups spinach and ricotta mixture

- 2 cups butternut squash purée

Instructions:

1. Prepare the Crust:

- Mix flour and salt. Cut in butter until the mixture resembles coarse crumbs. Add ice water until the dough comes together. Chill for 30 minutes.

2. Roll Out the Dough:

- Roll out two-thirds of the dough and fit it into a 9-inch pie dish. Chill. Roll out the remaining dough for the checkerboard top.

3. Prepare the Fillings:

- Make or warm the two fillings of your choice.

4. Assemble the Checkerboard:

- Use the remaining dough to create strips for the checkerboard pattern. Alternate the fillings in the pie dish, creating squares. Lay the dough strips over the filling, weaving them to form a lattice checkerboard.

5. Bake:

- Preheat oven to 375°F (190°C). Bake for 35–40 minutes, or until the crust is golden. Cool before serving.

Pro Tip: Use contrasting colors for maximum visual impact.

3. Decorative Lattice Fruit Pie

This classic pie showcases fresh fruit fillings and intricate latticework on the crust, making it perfect for seasonal celebrations.

Ingredients (Serves 8):

For the Crust:

- 2 1/2 cups all-purpose flour

- 1 teaspoon salt

- 1 tablespoon sugar

- 1 cup cold unsalted butter, cubed

- 6-8 tablespoons ice water

For the Filling:

- 4 cups mixed fruit (e.g., peaches, raspberries, blueberries)

- 1/2 cup granulated sugar

- 2 tablespoons cornstarch

- 1 tablespoon lemon juice

Instructions:

1. Prepare the Crust:

- Mix flour, salt, and sugar. Cut in butter until crumbly. Add ice water until the dough forms a ball. Chill for 30 minutes.

2. Prepare the Filling:

- Combine fruit, sugar, cornstarch, and lemon juice in a bowl. Toss to coat.

3. Assemble the Pie:

- Roll out the dough and fit it into a 9-inch pie dish. Pour in the fruit filling. Use the remaining dough to create a lattice top, braiding or weaving strips for an intricate design.

4. Bake:

- Preheat oven to 375°F (190°C). Bake for 40–45 minutes, or until the filling bubbles and the crust is golden. Cool before serving.

Pro Tip: Use small cookie cutters to add shapes, such as stars or leaves, to the lattice design.

Themed and Seasonal Pie Presentations

1. Seasonal Designs

- Spring: Use floral cutouts or pastel colors for Easter or Mother's Day pies.
    - Summer: Highlight fresh berries and bright colors for Fourth of July or garden parties.
    - Fall: Add leaf-shaped cutouts or use warm spices for Thanksgiving pies.
    - Winter: Incorporate snowflake designs or festive colors for holiday pies.

2. Themed Pies

- Birthdays: Create personalized pies with names or messages etched into the crust.
    - Weddings: Mini pies with monogrammed crusts make elegant wedding desserts.
    - Festivals: Use culturally significant patterns and colors to celebrate holidays like Diwali or Lunar New Year.

Tips for Success

1. Chill the Dough: Cold dough is easier to work with and holds its shape better during baking.

2. Use a Steady Hand: Take your time with intricate designs to ensure precision.

3. Test the Fillings: Ensure that the fillings are thick enough to hold their shape when cut.

4. Experiment with Shapes: Use cookie cutters, stencils, or freehand designs to create unique crusts.

Conclusion

Show-stopping party pies are a celebration of creativity, flavor, and craftsmanship. Whether you're layering colors for a rainbow pie, weaving a checkerboard pattern, or crafting intricate latticework, these pies are as much about the process as the end result. With the recipes, techniques, and ideas shared in this chapter, you'll be able to create pies that dazzle your guests and become the centerpiece of any occasion. Let's move forward to the final chapter, where we'll explore tips for hosting the ultimate pie party!

Chapter 15: Frozen and Ice Cream Pies

Frozen and ice cream pies are the perfect indulgence for warm weather or any time a refreshing, cool dessert is desired. These no-bake treats combine the simplicity of freezer-friendly preparation with the elegance and richness of layered flavors. Whether it's the creamy decadence of ice cream pie, the tangy sweetness of frozen strawberry cheesecake pie, or the bold flavors of mocha fudge pie, these recipes offer something for everyone.

This chapter will guide you through three delectable frozen pie recipes, techniques for layering fillings, and tips for slicing and serving these frozen delights like a pro.

Why Frozen and Ice Cream Pies?

1. Ease of Preparation

   - No baking is required, making these pies perfect for hot days when turning on the oven isn't an option.

2. Endless Flavor Possibilities

   - Frozen pies can be customized with any combination of flavors, from fresh fruits to rich chocolates and coffee.

   3. Make-Ahead Convenience

   - Frozen pies can be prepared days in advance, making them an excellent option for parties and gatherings.

Essential Techniques for Frozen and Ice Cream Pies

1. Choosing the Right Crust

- Cookie Crusts: Crushed cookies like Oreos, graham crackers, or gingersnaps are sturdy and complement frozen fillings.

- Nut-Based Crusts: Ground nuts mixed with butter and sugar create a crunchy, flavorful base.

- Pre-Made Crusts: Store-bought crusts offer convenience without compromising flavor.

2. Layering for Visual and Textural Appeal

- Use contrasting colors and textures for each layer.

- Allow each layer to freeze slightly before adding the next to ensure clean, distinct layers.

3. Freezing Tips

- Freeze the pie for at least 6–8 hours, or overnight, for the best texture.

- Cover the pie with plastic wrap or foil to prevent freezer burn.

4. Slicing and Serving Frozen Pies

- Use a sharp knife dipped in hot water for clean slices.

- Let the pie sit at room temperature for 5–10 minutes before slicing to soften slightly.

Recipes

1. Ice Cream Pie

This versatile dessert pairs a cookie crust with layers of your favorite ice cream flavors, topped with whipped cream and chocolate drizzle.

Ingredients (Serves 8):

For the Crust:

- 1 1/2 cups crushed Oreo cookies

- 6 tablespoons unsalted butter, melted

For the Filling:

- 1 pint vanilla ice cream, softened

- 1 pint chocolate ice cream, softened

For Topping:

- 1 cup whipped cream

- 1/4 cup chocolate syrup
- Chopped nuts or sprinkles

Instructions:

1. Prepare the Crust:

- Combine crushed Oreos and melted butter. Press the mixture into a 9-inch pie dish. Freeze for 15 minutes.

2. Layer the Ice Cream:

- Spread the vanilla ice cream evenly over the crust. Freeze for 30 minutes. Repeat with the chocolate ice cream, smoothing the top. Freeze for 2 hours.

3. Add Toppings:

- Before serving, spread whipped cream over the top. Drizzle with chocolate syrup and sprinkle with chopped nuts or sprinkles.

4. Serve:

- Let the pie sit at room temperature for 5 minutes before slicing.

Pro Tip: Experiment with different ice cream flavors, such as mint chocolate chip or strawberry, for a personalized twist.

2. Frozen Strawberry Cheesecake Pie

This frozen pie combines the creaminess of cheesecake with the bright, tangy flavor of strawberries for a refreshing summer treat.

Ingredients (Serves 8):

For the Crust:

- 1 1/2 cups crushed graham crackers
- 6 tablespoons unsalted butter, melted

For the Filling:

- 1 package (8 ounces) cream cheese, softened
- 1 cup Greek yogurt
- 1/2 cup powdered sugar
- 1 teaspoon vanilla extract
- 1 cup fresh strawberries, puréed
- 1/2 cup diced strawberries

For Topping:

- Fresh strawberries
- Whipped cream

Instructions:

1. Prepare the Crust:

- Combine graham cracker crumbs and melted butter. Press into a 9-inch pie dish. Freeze for 15 minutes.

2. Make the Filling:

- Beat cream cheese, yogurt, powdered sugar, and vanilla extract until smooth. Fold in strawberry purée and diced strawberries.

3. Assemble the Pie:

- Pour the filling into the crust and smooth the top. Freeze for at least 6 hours, or overnight.

4. Add Toppings:

- Before serving, garnish with fresh strawberries and dollops of whipped cream.

Pro Tip: Swirl additional strawberry purée on top for a decorative finish.

3. Mocha Fudge Pie

Rich and indulgent, this pie layers coffee ice cream with a velvety fudge topping, making it a dream dessert for coffee lovers.

Ingredients (Serves 8):

For the Crust:

- 1 1/2 cups crushed chocolate wafer cookies

- 6 tablespoons unsalted butter, melted

For the Filling:

- 1 pint coffee ice cream, softened

- 1/2 pint vanilla ice cream, softened

For the Fudge Layer:

- 1/2 cup heavy cream

- 1 cup dark chocolate chips

- 1 teaspoon espresso powder

For Topping:

- Whipped cream

- Chocolate shavings

Instructions:

1. Prepare the Crust:

- Mix crushed chocolate wafer cookies and melted butter. Press into a 9-inch pie dish. Freeze for 15 minutes.

2. Layer the Ice Cream:

- Spread coffee ice cream evenly over the crust. Freeze for 30 minutes. Add vanilla ice cream on top and smooth. Freeze for 2 hours.

3. Make the Fudge Layer:

- Heat heavy cream in a saucepan until simmering. Remove from heat and stir in chocolate chips and espresso powder until smooth. Let cool slightly, then pour over the frozen pie. Freeze for 1 hour.

4. Add Toppings:

- Before serving, decorate with whipped cream and chocolate shavings.

Pro Tip: Use decaffeinated coffee ice cream for a kid-friendly version.

Creative Variations

1. Seasonal Twists

- Use pumpkin spice ice cream for a fall-themed pie.

- Incorporate tropical fruits like mango or pineapple for a summer vibe.

2. Nut-Free and Dairy-Free Options

- Substitute nut-free cookies for the crust and use coconut or oat milk-based ice creams for the filling.

3. Themed Decorations

- Add food coloring to whipped cream for festive occasions, such as red and green for Christmas or pastel shades for Easter.

Tips for Success

1. Use a Springform Pan: For easy slicing and serving, assemble your frozen pie in a springform pan.

2. Chill Utensils: Keep your knife and serving spatula chilled to maintain the pie's shape when cutting.

3. Serve on Chilled Plates: Prevent the pie from melting too quickly by serving it on cold plates.

Conclusion

Frozen and ice cream pies are the ultimate no-bake desserts, combining creamy textures, vibrant flavors, and eye-catching presentations. Whether you're savoring the layered indulgence of an ice cream pie, the tangy brightness of a frozen strawberry cheesecake pie, or the bold richness of a mocha fudge pie, these recipes are sure to impress. With techniques for layering fillings, freezing, and serving, you'll master the art of creating frozen pies that are as delightful to look at as they are to eat. Celebrate the joy of frozen desserts and let these pies become your go-to treats for special occasions and everyday indulgences.

Conclusion: A Celebration of Pies

Pies hold a special place in the culinary world, transcending cultures, seasons, and occasions. They embody comfort, creativity, and tradition, blending artistry with practicality in a way few dishes can. From the first flaky crust to the last delicious crumb, pies are more than just food—they're a celebration of life's sweetest and most savory moments.

As we bring this journey to a close, this chapter will recap the techniques, recipes, and inspiration shared throughout this book. It will also serve as a final encouragement to experiment, innovate, and share the timeless joy of homemade pies with those you love.

The Journey Through Pie-Making

This book has been a comprehensive exploration of the art and science of pie-making, guiding you through foundational techniques, diverse recipes, and advanced skills. Let's revisit the highlights:

1. Mastering the Basics

- The Crust: From all-butter to gluten-free, mastering the crust was our first step. You learned how to achieve flakiness, tenderness, and structure with tips like keeping ingredients cold and handling dough minimally.

- Essential Tools: Rolling pins, pie weights, and crimping techniques were introduced to ensure professional-quality results at home.

2. Sweet Pies

- We explored classics like fruit pies, creamy custards, and decadent chocolate creations.

- Seasonal pies like pumpkin and pecan brought festive flavors to the table, while modern twists like rainbow and checkerboard pies showcased innovation.

3. Savory Pies

- From hearty pot pies to elegant quiches, savory pies proved their versatility as satisfying main courses.

- Techniques for balancing fillings and creating sturdy crusts were shared, ensuring savory pies could hold their own alongside their sweet counterparts.

4. Global and Creative Pies

- You ventured into global flavors with recipes for empanadas, steak and kidney pie, and tourtière.

- Creative presentations like decorative latticework and themed pies added artistry and personalization to your baking.

5. Alternative and Frozen Pies

- Gluten-free and vegan pies proved that dietary restrictions don't mean sacrificing flavor.

- Frozen pies like ice cream and mocha fudge pies demonstrated the refreshing appeal of freezer-friendly desserts.

Encouragement to Experiment

Pie-making is as much about personal expression as it is about following recipes. Here are some ways to continue evolving your skills and creativity:

1. Experiment with Ingredients

- Filling Variations: Swap out traditional fruits with tropical options like mango or passion fruit. Explore savory combinations like spiced lamb or curried vegetables.

- Crust Innovations: Incorporate herbs, spices, or even cheese into your crusts to complement your fillings.

2. Play with Presentation

- Latticework: Add color and contrast to your lattice designs by using dyed or layered dough.

- Shapes and Stamps: Use cookie cutters or hand-cut shapes to create themed decorations for your pies.

3. Explore New Techniques

- Layering Flavors: Combine contrasting textures, like creamy custards with crunchy toppings, to surprise your palate.

- Infusions: Add depth to your pies by infusing creams or syrups with herbs, spices, or teas.

The Timeless Joy of Sharing Pies

At their core, pies are meant to be shared. They bring people together, turning ordinary moments into cherished memories. Whether it's a warm apple pie fresh from the oven or an intricately crafted checkerboard pie at a festive gathering, pies have a way of fostering connection.

1. Pies as Gifts

- A homemade pie is a heartfelt gift that shows care and effort. Personalize it with unique flavors or decorative touches to make it extra special.

2. Pies at Celebrations

- Pies are perfect for birthdays, weddings, and holidays, offering endless customization to match the occasion.

3. Everyday Moments

- Don't wait for a special occasion—sharing a simple pie with loved ones can turn an ordinary day into something extraordinary.

Final Reflections

Pie-making is a journey, one that combines technical skill with creativity and love. As you continue on this journey, remember that:

1. Imperfection Is Beautiful

- A slightly uneven crust or a bit of filling bubbling over the edge doesn't diminish the joy or flavor of a homemade pie.

2. Each Pie Tells a Story

- Every pie you bake carries a piece of your personality, your memories, and your love. It's a gift you give to yourself and others.

3. The Journey Is Never Over

- There are always new techniques to try, flavors to explore, and designs to master. Pie-making is a lifelong art.

Inspiration to Keep Baking

Pies are as versatile as they are delicious. Let this book serve as a foundation for your pie-making adventures, inspiring you to create:

- A pie for every season: Celebrate the bounty of spring, the freshness of summer, the warmth of autumn, and the comfort of winter with seasonal ingredients.

- A pie for every palate: From classic favorites to bold innovations, pies can cater to every taste and dietary need.

- A pie for every story: Whether it's a cherished family recipe or a new creation, every pie has a story to tell.

Conclusion: Celebrating Pies Together

As you close this book, take with you the skills, recipes, and inspiration to create pies that delight, comfort, and bring people together. Whether you're baking a simple fruit pie for a quiet evening or crafting a show-stopping creation for a grand celebration, know that you're part of a timeless tradition.

The joy of pie-making lies not only in the final product but also in the process—the mixing, rolling, filling, and sharing. It's an act of love, creativity, and connection that transcends time and place.

So, roll out your dough, gather your favorite ingredients, and let the magic of pie-making unfold in your kitchen. Celebrate the art, the craft, and the heart of pies, and may every slice bring a little more happiness to your table.

Happy baking!

Don't miss out!

Visit the website below and you can sign up to receive emails whenever Olivia Bennett publishes a new book. There's no charge and no obligation.

https://books2read.com/r/B-A-QLEKD-QXKAG

BOOKS 2 READ

Connecting independent readers to independent writers.

About the Author

Olivia Bennett is a celebrated food writer and chef with expertise spanning multiple culinary disciplines. With a passion for making home cooking accessible, she specializes in guiding readers through everything from hearty casseroles to delicate pastries. Her work is known for its clear instructions, practical tips, and deep understanding of both traditional and modern cooking techniques.